The **LAW** of the **Vital FEW**

How to do more by doing less

Anthony Sanni

Tellwell Talent
www.tellwell.ca

ISBN
978-1-7773257-1-8 (Hardcover)
978-1-7773257-3-2 (Paperback)
978-1-7773257-2-5 (eBook)

For Sophia and Sterling

TABLE OF CONTENTS

The wheel is ranked by many as the most important invention of all time. And by important, they mean it was the invention that made the most impact on civilization. It's hard to argue with that—there's a reason why the cliché "don't reinvent the wheel" persists even today, some thirty-five hundred years after the wheel was invented.

The invention of the wheel was a major advance for human culture for many reasons. First, it's a truly original human creation because it arose without an analog in nature that was copied. That is, there were no wheels on earth until man invented them. But beyond its humble form of a simple, spherical disc, it's what the wheel allowed us to do that is truly amazing—the *possibilities* it opened up. The wheel changed everything.

Waterwheels drove irrigation, wagon wheels drove immigration. The wheel gave birth to the pulley and the gear in all their variations—they were used to build machines and machines built our civilization.

The wheel was the disruptive technology of the ancient times that allowed us to do something that sounded counterintuitive— move more weight with less effort. In other words, the wheel allowed us to multiply the output of our work without increasing the effort we applied to that work. In fact, it often resulted in using *less* effort than before. It's easier to roll a crate on wheels than it is to heave the same crate.

Indeed, it's hard to imagine there was ever a world without wheels, gears, or pulleys.

But it's not hard to see that many of us still act as though we can only get more value and enjoyment out of life through the *volume* of our work. That is, how *much* work we do.

The idea we explore in this book—the Law of the Vital Few—turns that on its head. It contends that *where* we give is more important than how *much* we give. It shows us we can get, have, be and give so much more by directing our energy away from the many trivial pursuits that drain us and focusing squarely on the Vital Few that move us in the direction of our goals and aspirations.

We can do more, not by doing more as conventional wisdom might suggest, but by doing *less*.

In this book, we will focus on what this means for us and how we can make adjustments to use this law to our advantage. We will see how a vital few factors—activities, qualities, and relationships—exert a disproportionately large effect on the output and outcomes of our lives. And how relatively few factors are responsible for most of our troubles.

We will explore the core principle of the Law of the Vital Few, which I distill simply as the statement: Only a few things really matter, but the few that matter, matter a lot.

The Vital Few (TVF) influences so many aspects of our lives; from the deeply meaningful—like how most of our results can be traced to a small number of activities; to the rather trivial and bizarre—like how most of the exclamation marks in current US president Donald Trump's posts on Twitter can be traced to relatively few tweets.

At its core, TVF is an old idea with renewed relevance in this modern age where there are simultaneously more distractions and opportunities than there have ever been in human history. Now more than ever we need to look again at what our Vital Few are, otherwise, we will get swept away by tides of triviality. We need to look at where and how we are investing our time, energy, and resources—in a word, our lives.

As you'll see, I did not come up with the core idea of the Vital Few. Perhaps as a testament to its widespread influence, the idea has been called many names by different thinkers in different fields of study over time. But here, I take the concept beyond the realm of a "cool idea" to impress people over cocktails in bars or charts in boardrooms, and into the realm of reach for direct applicability in the day to day life of the individual—you and I.

This book provides a clear way to look at our lives in the light of TVF. It also provides tools for finding and engaging with the Vital Few that make the difference in our lives. I have applied its principles in my work as a coach and consultant helping individuals and organizations direct their efforts to the vital few factors and activities that make the biggest impact on their goals. And now, I am happy to share those principles with you.

I invite you to explore this revolutionary idea and its profound implications for transforming your life. Hopefully, it gets the wheels turning to bring about a positive revolution for good in your life and empowers you to do more by doing less, just like the wheel did for humanity.

BOOK I

THE LAW OF THE VITAL FEW, AND YOU

Our greatest gains are traceable to a small number of sources. So are our greatest losses.

The Law of the Vital Few is simple but profound. It's also counterintuitive. The notion that a lot of what consumes our efforts produces little to no returns can be difficult to grasp and accept. But once realized, it can be a powerful force for positive change.

Here we expound on the idea of the Law of the Vital Few —its origins and different manifestations. More importantly, we discuss what it means for you and how it can utterly transform your life for the better.

CHAPTER 1

The Vital Few: An Old and New Concept

Before we can begin to apply The Law of The Vital Few to our lives and work, it helps to understand the concept itself. That's what this chapter is about. This foundation is useful and interesting, but it is not vital to your use of the law. If you'd rather skip this chapter, go right ahead. I promise I won't get mad. But if you'd like to learn some of the background of this law, as well as feast your eyes on a few lovely charts, then read on.

The Law of the Vital Few first made its appearance as the Pareto Principle in the 1800s. It would go on to reappear under different monikers and with slight variations and applications from the Principle of Least Effort to the 80-20 Principle popularized in recent times in Richard Koch's aptly titled book, *The 80/20 Principle*.

My personal favourite is the one I have chosen for this book—the Law of the Vital Few. I first encountered it in the work of Moses Juran, who was greatly influential in the Quality Movement that transformed the Japanese automobile industry into the global force it is today. He demonstrated through his work that the greatest improvements to the efficiency and effectiveness of a system can be obtained by making changes to relatively few parameters. Conversely, most inefficiencies in a system can be traced to relatively few factors. He is quoted as saying, "80% of problems are the result of only 20% of activities."

This insight was a big part of his approach to quality management and is still a large part of the practice today.

The core idea that all these terms—the Pareto Principle, the Law of Least Effort, the 80/20 Principle, or the Law of the Vital Few—have in common is this:

There is an inherent imbalance in a system between the ratio of inputs to outputs with a tendency for relatively few inputs to account for a disproportionately large ratio of outputs.

NORMAL, PARETO AND POWER LAW

The normal way of looking at life takes a fairly average view and is a big part of our social conversations. We speak of average students, and people with average means or abilities—the Joes and Janes of the world. Appropriately, in statistics, data distributions where the average values dominate are called "normal" distributions—such as height or weight for example. Since most of us tend to think this way, it may be a good starting point to compare "normal" to "power" distributions. Or, what I like to call comparing bells to tails.

Without geeking out on the math and stats, in a normal distribution, the mass of values build up from the left (lesser values) to a peak in the middle and then drops off again to the right (larger values) like a wave. Values close to the middle (the mean, or average) are more common and so most of the "mass" of values are in the middle, resulting in the familiar "bell" curve—a common pattern in statistics.

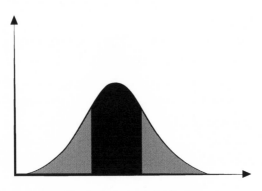

Figure: Bell curve distribution

Population height typically follows a normal distribution. If you plot height, say, in inches along the horizontal axis and the number of people of that height in the population along the vertical axis, you will end up with most people being in the "average height" region—the middle of the curve around the middle of the horizontal height axis.

There are a few really tall people to the right and a few really short people to the left, but most are in the middle—people of average height. But not everything follows a normal distribution. In fact, some really important aspects of life deviate drastically from this normal pattern. Introducing a central character in the evolution of the Law of the Vital Few...

The curious 19th century engineer

In 1896, an Italian engineer turned economist developed an interesting curiosity. He wondered if he could apply his great skill with data and statistics to study the distribution of wealth among the population; could the numbers reveal anything interesting?

At the time, economics was largely a social science almost completely innocent of any mathematical sophistication. It definitely wasn't the graph-and-chart-speckled discipline we know it as today. So, applying his stellar analytical skills, he gathered the data and ran the numbers.

His results revealed something unexpected. He found that roughly 80% of the land belonged to about 20% of the population. There was a marked imbalance in distribution with most resources belonging to a relatively small number of people. And even though his discovery was made in the 19th century, the phenomenon persists today with regular references both in academic literature and everyday discourse to the affluent "one percent" who hold or earn most of the wealth and income.

The engineer's name? Vilfredo Pareto, founder of the eponymous Pareto Principle mentioned earlier. The principle says that 80 percent of results come from 20 percent of efforts. More precisely, it suggests an inherent imbalance in a system between the ratio of inputs to outputs with a tendency for relatively few inputs to account for a disproportionately large ratio of outputs. And even though Pareto might not have used the term at the time, his observation hinted at the existence of a Power Law.

Raised to the power

The Power Law is a term used to describe an occurrence where a small number of factors account for a disproportionately large effect—negative or positive.

Let us recall our normal distribution where the peak was in the middle of the bell. Well, the characteristic feature of the Power Law distribution is that the peak is *not* in the middle. Instead, it's at the edge and then falls off in dramatic fashion. Most of the "mass" is at one end of the curve with a steep drop from that point. This leads to the observed long "tail" displayed by this distribution.

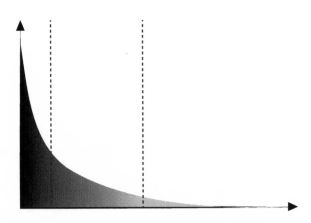

Figure: Power Law Distribution (The Long-Tail)

As Pareto observed, this is the typical distribution of wealth. Indeed, the 80/20 principle, which is a common name for Pareto's principle, is just a special kind of Power Law—one in which 80% of the entire mass of the values is concentrated in a 20% section of the distribution. The rest of it forms the long tail at the end.

To contrast the bells and tails, if we took that exact same population that had a normal bell curve distribution for height and plotted their income, we would end up with a tail-type curve. That is, most of the income and wealth would be held by a few people (the first part of the curve). That income would then dramatically taper off to those with very little (the long tail).

Unlike height, speaking of "average" income really makes no sense because there are a few people with so much more money than others that their individual "mass" would skew the results.

For example, if things were "normal" and we have three people who each made $10k, $15k and $20k a year, their average income would be $15k/year. That is, $10k + $15k + $20k = $45k (the total amount of money earned) divided by the number of people. In this case three. So, we have $45k/3 = $15k. Which is ok really—it *does* approximate the reality of this highly simplified population.

But what is more likely, based on what we now know about income distribution, is that about 90% of the total $45k made would go to only one of them. Then roughly $3k would go to the next and only $1k to the last—in keeping with the Power Law. You would still have an "average" of $15K between the three, but this would be useless to work with as a representation of the reality if you were, say, planning a social project or trying to set a price for a product to sell to them.

Statisticians cleverly deal with this problem by speaking of "median" income. The median quantity—which takes the income at the exact middle of the distribution—is a better representation of the reality than a calculated average value. In our simplified income distribution, the median income would be $3k which is nowhere near the mathematical average of $15k. It is, however, more reflective of reality.

For normal distributions like height, this is a non-issue because the median would closely approximate average (the peak of the bell). But with the Power Law, it's a very different story, as we have seen here. In fact, in the Power Law distribution, there is no normal. The distribution is both factually and metaphorically *abnormal*.

It is this abnormality that we are concerned with in this book and how it manifests in different aspects of life and business. The observed imbalance that results is widely expressed in 80/20 terms. Indeed, Richard Koch opted for this as the title of his book for the reason of simplicity. However, as he also noted, like all things in nature, there is no perfect symmetry in this ratio.

The numbers do not always split perfectly into 80 and 20. And as tempting as it may be to assume otherwise, they do not always add up to 100. For example, the prevalent magazine *Popular Science* recently published an article stating that about 1/5th (20%) of Americans are responsible for about half (50%) of the country's food emissions. The sum of 50 and 20 is 70, not 100. That is because each of those numbers (50 and 20) are percentages of two different things (population and emissions).

I think Koch puts it nicely when he says:

> To apply the 80/20 principle, you have to have two sets of data, both adding up to 100 percent, and one measuring a variable quantity owned, exhibited, or caused by the people or things making up the other 100 percent.

For our example of food emissions, this would translate as 20% (out of 100%) of Americans are responsible for 50% (out of 100%) of food emissions. Thus, yielding a 50/20 relationship; 50% of emissions come from 20% of the American population.

The takeaway here is that we should not think about expressions of 80/20 or the Vital Few in percentage terms. These are *not* percentages, they are *relationships*. They express how much influence one part of a system has on the overall (or another) system. The total of all inputs will still add up to 100 (that is what a total is after all), but the *relationship* between the vital few inputs and their corresponding outputs need not add up to 100 at all. Yet even when the relationship is not as tidy as adding up to a hundred percent, it still provides insights that can guide efforts and drive gains.

Imagine a company producing ten products—A, B, C, D, E, F, G, H, I & J. In the simplest case of even distribution of output, one would expect these products to return 10% each and add up nicely to 100%. People with more experience in business would expect something different, but maybe not too different—perhaps one product doing very well, then a close second, and so on to the least performing product.

Keeping things simple, let's assign this in alphabetical order so that product A is the top seller.

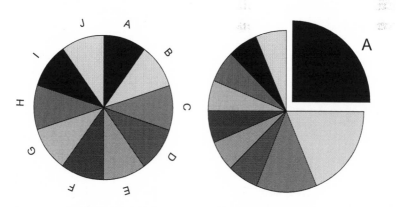

Figure: Profit from products based on even distribution and top-seller product A

However, after a business analysis, the company may find that 59% of profits come from a single product, say, product A, which makes up only 10% of its offerings.[1]

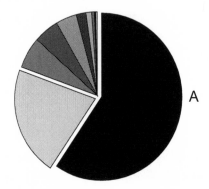

Figure: Profit from product A accounting for 59% of profits

The mathematically inclined will notice that those numbers add up to 69, not 100. Adding up all the company's profits from products A through J still gets us to 100% of course. But this relationship between what percentage of the products (inputs) are vital and how much they contribute to the total profit (output) do not need to, and rarely actually do add up to 100.

But this doesn't affect the usefulness of the information at all. As much as we might find it satisfying to always have the relationships add up to a nice, round figure, that would be missing the point. The point is that the relationship gives us insight into the factors that hold the most sway on outcomes.

Not only does this needn't add up to 100 but sometimes it can, in fact, exceed it. For example, 20% of inputs may account for 90% of outputs, adding up to 110. And other times, it may not even come close but still provide immense insight.

---

[1] Note that product A may not be a single product but may be an entire segment or suite of products. An educational institution may find, for example, that 59% of its profits come from small, tailored on-site seminars vs mass-market online offerings or generic in-class courses.

To make things more interesting, the relationship can also be so extremely skewed to the point of being mind-boggling. For example, in the English language, with its approximate vocabulary of 250,000 words, a measly 100 words make up about 50% of spoken language. In case you are wondering, "measly" isn't one of them. As a percentage, this means that 0.04% of words in the English language make up about 50% (or half) of all speech.

That is an extremely small portion exerting a ludicrously large pull on the whole. This trend is observed by linguists in other languages too.

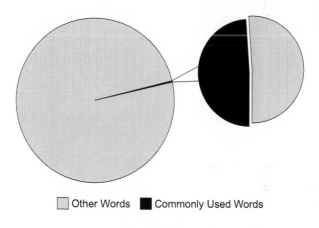

Other Words ■ Commonly Used Words

Figure: Relationship between percentage of words to
most commonly used words in language[2]

Clearly, only a few words matter, but they matter a lot. Again, the sum of 0.04 and 50 tells us nearly nothing. But the *relationship* between 0.04 and 50 tells us a whole lot! If we were learning a new language, that singular insight would save us a lot of time and effort. Chapter 12 provides recommendations on learning using this principle.

---

[2] In the figure above, the portion for 0.04 was so thin that it would not have appeared in print. What you see is actually a 10X multiplication to 0.4%

But going back to our business example, even though the relationship of numbers for product A does not neatly add up to 100, that company had better take a closer look at product A. It definitely is a part of that company's Vital Few by the sheer disproportionality between its relative size and the impact it has on profits.

For a single product making up only 10% of offerings to account for 59% of profits is a big deal, awkward sums aside.

This example is more than hypothetical. Thinking in terms of the Vital Few has shaped multi-billion-dollar corporate strategies. Consider Procter and Gamble (P&G), the world's largest household products maker. In 2014, then CEO Alan George Lafley made a bold strategic move to cut back on growing the company's brand portfolio and instead focus on the 80 brands that generated 95% of the company's profits and 90% of its sales.

At the time, the company was carrying 180 brands. In 80/20 relationship terms, 44% of its brands accounted for 95% of its profits—a 95/44 relationship. These brands were P&G's Vital Few, and their leader decided to leverage them instead of spreading their efforts thin across a broader brand base.

The company initiated a process of paring down to focus and the strategy has helped P&G weather the tumultuous economic environment of recent years while staying profitable and consistently increasing dividend payouts to shareholders year after year, according to its annual reports.

THE LAW OF THE VITAL FEW: BEYOND NUMBERS AND STATISTICS TO ACTION

In general, I try *not* to think in sums and statistics too much when it comes to the Vital Few. I find it distracting. Instead, I focus on the relationships and how much impact a factor (or related group of factors) exerts on the whole, so I can gauge just how influential it is and how the insight can help me or my clients do more by doing less.

This is one of the reasons why I won't spend a lot of time on numerical analysis but on practical and actionable ideas. It's also why I have opted for the term the Vital Few. It takes us away from a strictly numerical mindset—fussing over numbers and ratios—to a reflective and action-oriented mindset. It has an imminence to it, a call to action embedded in it. It asks us to find *our* Vital Few. Sure, empirical data helps, but it's what the data tells us that matters the most.

While all the possible combinations of numbers and ratios may cause frantic head-scratching, and the idea of least effort may conjure up (albeit erroneously) thoughts of laziness, the Vital Few idea is easy to grasp. It captures the essence of this powerful and transformative principle plainly and effectively.

As I have coined it in this book, the Law of the Vital Few says simply, *a few things matter, but the few that matter, matter a lot.* It's a call to find what those few things are and then to give ourselves more to them. And by doing that, we get more out of life and work—to enjoy and give back.

VITAL ACTIVITIES

The word "activity" is used so often that we don't really think about what it means. But once its meaning settles in for you, as it did for me, you may find that your view and choices about your activities shift. The "act" part is easy enough to understand. It's related to action and simply means "doing". No surprises there. It's the "vit" part that might interest you.

Vit is an old Latin word meaning "life" or "living". It shows up in words like revitalize (to give life again), vitality (being alive), and, you guessed it, vital. In fact, the word *activus,* from which we get "active" has philosophical origins recorded as far back as the 16th century and means "liveliness". We should look at activity very differently. It's more than something we simply do, it's something we create.

Every activity we take part in creates a dynamic between action and life energy. This dynamic can be positive; that is, the actions enhance our lifeforce. Or the dynamic can be negative; that is, the activity depletes our lifeforce either in quantity or quality. Like credit cards or cheques give direction to money, activity gives direction to life energy. Sometimes we spend, sometimes we squander. But what we really want to do is *invest*.

So, the question becomes: Which activities create a positive dynamic and which do not? In other words, what are good activity investments?

The particulars will differ from person to person. A professional soccer player will invest heavily in the activity of vigorous physical training for hours a day while a writer may require only a few hours a week. The writer though, should spend many hours writing— likely more than the soccer player may care for. In other words, a day in the life of a successful writer and star soccer player will look very different on the surface. The same goes for successful doctors, software developers, stay-at-home parents, entrepreneurs, teachers, musicians, and so on. But though appearing diverse on the surface, a closer look at each of these cases often reveals intriguing patterns that show a mastery of how energy is invested wisely in the right activities to produce the observed success.

You too can create or enhance your success by paying attention to your activities (more on this later). By redirecting your energy from less effective activities to the Vital Few, you will be doing less, but achieving more, and enhancing your vitality in the process.

Is TVF unfair?

A question might have surfaced in your mind at this point: Is this fair?

We somehow expect effort to be democratic—the majority rule—essentially, normal. Output should be a result of sheer number. This seems equitable; majority carries the vote, just like it does in democratic governance. Of course, even in politics, it's never this simple.

The reality is there are a small number of people in virtually any group who hold most of the power. From families to countries, this holds true. In a nuclear family, it's the parents. And in countries, it's a relatively small group of leaders.

You might say those leaders were voted in by a majority, ergo, democratic. But the truth is, there are often unseen power groups, kingmakers, and even puppet-masters behind the scenes. At its extreme, this results in a full-fledged oligarchy where a handful of people unilaterally decide the fate of the state. Otherwise, as with the democratic states, elected officials and lawmakers bear the responsibility of governance with more accountability, but still with power that is far from the representation of an "average".

So, the question remains—and it is one that I have also pondered—is it fair that a few factors should influence so many? Is it fair that a few people should, like Pareto discovered, control most of the resources or hold most of the power?

After some introspection, I have found that the answer is: It doesn't matter. The question is a distraction.

TVF simply *is*.

To think in TVF terms means accepting with open eyes, the inherent imbalance of influence. Whether that be the influence of certain activities over others in achieving our goals or the influence of certain people over the experience and outcomes of our lives— the most important of whom is ourselves.

Once you have accepted this, you can proceed to move forward *with* the principle to where the real work lies—identifying those pivotal practices and people. Without it, we find ourselves spending precious time and energy on pursuits that yield little returns, the whole time sacrificing those efforts that could move us in the direction of our goals and dreams faster and easier.

Once we have made our peace with TVF, we can get to work using it for our good and the good of those around us.

CHAPTER 2

Manifestations of The Vital Few

The popular sister process-efficiency methodologies of Lean and Six Sigma were at one time engaged in a serious case of sibling rivalry. The Lean methodology—based on the Japanese principles of Kaizen (continuous improvement)—was a big part of the quality movement that had helped Japanese companies, over many decades, make huge strides in both process efficiency and quality of output.

As early as 1870, manufacturing businesses in the US were already seeing encroachment by Japanese competitors—Japanese companies were producing better products more efficiently than their American counterparts. Six Sigma was created by Motorola in the US around 1987 to respond to its loss of ground in the market to the compelling high-quality, low-price offerings of the Japanese entrants.

And so, the rivalry was born with the younger, impetuous sibling ceaselessly struggling to catch up to her older, more experienced sister.

Both methodologies would finally reconcile into what is known today as Lean Six Sigma. The principles of this combined method draw on the key strengths of each—the first, Lean, emphasizing reduction of waste; and the second, Six Sigma, emphasizing the elimination of defects (also waste).

It probably won't surprise you to discover that the fundamental idea behind the Law of The Vital Few is at play in key aspects of the individual methods as well as the juxtaposed Lean Six Sigma approach to organizational efficiency. If your company were ever to hire a consultant in this field, one of the documents they would deliver in their final report package is a Pareto Chart. The chart is an embodiment of The Vital Few thinking illustrated visually.

I was once involved in a Six Sigma analysis for an educational institution that was looking to streamline its curriculum management process. The institution had identified a problem— their curriculum administration was consuming a huge amount of human and, consequently, financial resources.

The current process was painfully slow and produced many interpersonal and inter-departmental conflicts. Of course, all this resulted in the institution spending more than it needed or was willing to on this aspect of the business.

So, they enlisted the help of a Six Sigma Blackbelt. This doesn't mean this person could kick really high or take you on in a street fight—it meant that he was experienced enough in the principles of Six Sigma to lead a large project. I have always wondered why these folks are called Blackbelts. I guess Jedi Master was taken.

I was brought in for my knowledge of Lean and my previous experience with the institution—no sexy titles for me. I would have appreciated Lean Machine, but I don't make the rules.

We got to work and one of the results of the exercise was, as you might have you guessed, a Pareto Chart detailing the processes that accounted for the largest drain on people's time. It also probably won't surprise you that there were relatively few— the Vital Few—processes that were causing most of the waste and heartache.

With a few tweaks to the workflows and software, the process was drastically improved with all metrics showing an average of 40% improvement. What's interesting here is not the result per se, but the fact that these results were achieved by only a few minor tweaks. The improvements were neither particularly difficult nor expensive to execute once the Vital Few culprits were identified.

Though I quite enjoy black belts myself (more for holding my pants up), you do not need to become, wear, or even own a black belt to apply this powerful concept to your life. It is really about first accepting the truth that large and complex problems do not always need large and complex solutions—they may just need changes in a relatively small number of areas.

The real work of business and life is to find what those small areas are, those vital few factors that wield the quiet but potent power to change everything, for better or for worse, and then to strive to change them for the better.

If you do decide to buy or become a black belt, you might be happy you did—both are extremely versatile.

THE VITAL FEW AND THE INTERNET INFLUENCER CULTURE

The rise of the internet and connectivity has made it possible, now more than ever, to reach other people. As of mid-2019, it was estimated that over half the population of the world are internet users—some 4.3 billion people. This is up from a paltry 1.8 billion only 10 years ago. That's an increase of about 230% in internet users over the course of a decade. World population, on the other hand, only increased by 10% within the same time frame. The trend has been upward since data started being collected in 1995.

So clearly, more and more people are gaining access to the internet.

That's great for all of us, right? With a doubling of the users, there should be a doubling of the useful content, right?

I'm sure by now you are shaking your head in anticipation of the truth. This brings us to an interesting phenomenon marketers call the 90-9-1 rule. If that looks a little bit like a restatement of the Law of the Vital Few, well, keep reading.

Analysis conducted by the global user experience research firm Nielsen Norman shows that contribution to the internet follows the 90-9-1 pattern. That is, 90% of users are consumers (what Nielsen Norman calls lurkers), 9% contribute nominally, and 1% account for most of the contributions.

In the online world, the gap between consumption and contribution can be a chasm. The firm's insightful article on "participation inequality" states that for Wikipedia—one of the most popular sites on the internet that allows users to contribute, edit, and consume content—only 68,000 (0.2%) of the 32 million users at the time of the study contributed at all.

Drilling down further, only about 1,000 people (0.003%) accounted for more than 60% of the content on the site.

The article states:

> Wikipedia's most active 1,000 people—0.003% of its users—contribute about two-thirds of the site's edits. Wikipedia is thus even more skewed than blogs, with a 99.8-0.2-0.003 rule.

Users   Contributions

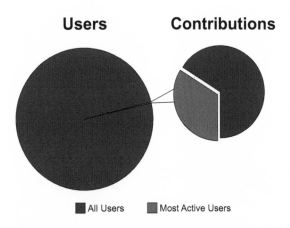

■ All Users   ■ Most Active Users

Figure: Wikipedia users and contribution[3]

What does this mean for the people on Wikipedia? Well, if you are one of the 1,000, you have a staggering influence over what the 32 million users see on the site. You could say you're a Wikipedia Influencer. Or, in our terms, you are one of the Vital

---

[3] In the figure, the portion for 0.003 was so thin that it would not have appeared in print. What you see is actually a 100X multiplication to 0.3%

Few for Wikipedia and what you say counts, a lot! This is true not just for Wikipedia, but for internet communities in general.

Even our offline communities show this phenomenon of imbalance. You will admit that some people in our communities create and contribute more than others; that some have more influence on how things go than others. What we see with online communities is a reflection of our offline communities. Lurkers and consumers as well as influencers and creators have always been and will likely always be with us.

Savvy marketers now use this 90-9-1 rule to drive profits powered by the internet. Sponsored videos and articles by charismatic personalities with large followings on social media and streaming services like YouTube are abundant. Affiliate purchase links attached to these influencers ensure the marketers can track their return on investment (ROI) on influencer marketing and on and on it goes. Influence now has an accurate dollar value. And the Vital Few influencers are driving and reaping a disproportionate share of the gains.

Now, you might argue that influence based on online content contribution via the 90-9-1 rule is novel and flawed. That the algorithms in search engines that run on metrics of how much content is produced as well as how much the content is consumed and shared enhance how much influencers are "in our faces" and thus increase their influence by a kind of snowball effect.

But these algorithms and the limelight they shine are really no different than, say, an editor's picks or the bestsellers list on the shelves of your local bookstore. Or a newspaper's choice to cover the 5,000-man rally over the 50-man assembly. The internet has only revealed us more measurably to ourselves. At least as far as this phenomenon of imbalance of influence, impact, and value is concerned.

It has shown us starkly, numerically, that the greatest value online can be traced to a relatively small number of sources. Similarly, in our lives, the greatest value can often be traced to a relatively small number of "Influencers". These may very well be people just like our internet influencers but they can also be aspects of ourselves that produce disproportionately higher value than others. Finding and tapping into these can make all the difference.

The two examples given so far in this chapter—Lean-Six Sigma Methodology and Internet Influence—are meant to illustrate two vital principles that have the power to completely change and improve our lives. And because it bears repeating:

Most of our problems can be traced to a vital few sources. Most of our value and benefit originates from a vital few sources.

Stated as one: A few things matter, but the few that matter, matter a lot!

THE VITAL FEW AND BLACK DRESSES: THE STORY OF QUINCY APPAREL

In the fall of 2011, a pair of Harvard MBAs—Christina Wallace and Alex Nelson—conceived of a business born out of a frustration they both felt. Both women, rather tall and slender, struggled to find office clothes that fit well.

Shopping for flattering clothes was difficult. *Why was this so hard?* They wondered. In their research, they discovered that sizing for women's clothes in the United States was based on grossly outdated models from the 1940s. These old models of sizing assumed an hourglass figure with dimensions and ratios that simply did not cater to the more diverse reality of women's figures. In fact, they found that this model catered to only about 8% of US women.

They also found that the office apparel industry for women was split into two levels. On the first level tier were brands priced reasonably but had a bad fit. On the upper-tier stood high-fashion brands that provided better fit but were priced beyond the reach of most consumers. In short, they discovered that a large portion of the population was under-served in the area of well-fitting, affordable office apparel.

They had identified a space in the women's office wear market where they could play—a reasonably-priced, better-fitting, decent quality line of office clothing for the modern woman. Christina Wallace and Alex Nelson created the brand Quincy Apparel to fill this gap. And after many rounds of market research, consultations, product testing, and raising capital, Quincy Apparel launched later that year with a production run to fulfill trunk show orders they had collected.

Over the next few months, revenues saw steady growth. Here was a great business idea filling a real need, beginning what seemed poised to be a successful run.

This is why you might not have predicted what happened next. In January of 2013, just over two years after the business plan for Quincy Apparel was written, the business shut down. For good.

Why was this? The Harvard Business Review (HBR) case study states:

> Quincy's value proposition had appeal: sales growth had been strong. However, due to Quincy's sizing scheme, inventory was high and operations were complex. Operational challenges made it difficult to consistently deliver better fit, and merchandise return rates were high.

It was this last point that caught my eye—merchandise return rates were high. My TVF senses started tingling. I dove into the data and sure enough, there it was in a table in the HBR case study titled "Customer Segments: Ordering Patterns".

Take a look at the table below and see if you can spot it:

Segment	% Customers	Avg. Order (Net of Returns)	Orders/ Year	% Merchandise Returns
Affluent Traditionalists	14%	$650	2-4	7%
Rising Stars	32%	$300	2-4	6%
Trend Seekers	32%	$145	1-2	11%
Fit Skeptics	22%	$5	1	85%

Figure: Quincy Apparel Customer Segments: Ordering
Patterns (Reproduced with Permission)

Did you catch it lurking in the bottom row? 85% of merchandise returns came from just 22% of the customers. Even more interestingly, this customer segment—The Fit Skeptics—not only accounted for the highest number of goods returned, but they also accounted for the lowest value of orders. In other words, most of Quincy's costly returns (and lowest value) were coming from a relatively small segment of customers (the Vital Few).

On the other side, the customer segment called the "Affluent Traditionalists" not only accounted for the lowest returns but they also accounted for the largest value of $650 versus $5 from the Fit Skeptics. In other words, most of Quincy Apparel's revenue (and overall profit) was coming from a relatively small segment of customers (the Vital Few).

Now, there are many complex reasons why a business might fail, and Quincy Apparel was no exception. Some of the other factors were already alluded to in the earlier paragraph from the HBR case analysis. And other sources like Business Insider have suggested that an investor behaviour trend of the period—where there was an unwillingness to invest larger sums to get start-ups past the initial stages—played a role in Quincy Apparel folding up.

However, considering that the rate of merchandise purchased and then returned was a major factor, it's hard not to speculate that had Quincy's leadership recognized and addressed this manifestation of TVF, they would have improved the company's chances of survival. What difference might it have made, I wonder, if Quincy had focused on the Affluent Traditionalists—their Vital Few—and sought to expand and serve that segment more while simultaneously developing methods to reduce the participation and impact of Fit Skeptics? Would the outcome have been different?

Hindsight, as they say, is 20/20 (or 80/20 in this case), but the takeaway here is clear—ignoring the vital few sources of both good and grief in our affairs can be a recipe for failure. It may not be the *only* thing that could hamper our success, but it surely is a critical one.

CHAPTER 3

Finding Your Vital Few

The quality of your life is a direct reflection of the
quality of the questions you are asking yourself
Anthony Robbins

When I started my coaching business, I tried all kinds of things to attract clients. I got a few here and there but not at the frequency I wanted. I was passionate about helping people overcome barriers to being productive and communicating their value effectively. But passion alone was not enough.

All this was further complicated by the fact that I still had my day job and a growing family. At one point, I was on the verge of a breakdown when my wife and I decided to take a vacation to cool off and regroup.

When I returned from the trip, I was refreshed, but not much had changed. On top of that, we discovered my wife was pregnant. It was exciting but scary because I could foresee life was about to get even busier. Clearly, I couldn't continue to do everything I was already doing trying to grow my business, there just weren't enough hours in the day. I had to do a few things—the right few. The Vital Few. But what few?

How I chose the few things that I focused on is what I want to share with you in this chapter. As they did for me, the next few questions will set you on your path to isolating the most promising pursuits worthy of your precious time and energy. These questions apply as much to organizations as they do to individuals. Once you start asking these questions, you will discover that you already have most of the answers—you just never asked.

1. WHAT AM I GOOD AT?

Everyone is good at something, and the same goes for companies. Based on our unique combination of nature and nurture, we are able to do some things better than others. Our nature is a result of our genes buzzing away quietly in the background; our nurture is how we were raised, our accumulated experiences, and our environment over the course of our lives. These two forces of nature and nurture are the unsung ingredients of what is commonly referred to as "talent".

Nature is legendary swimmer Michael Phelps' favourable physique. Standing at a limber 6ft 4 (1.9m), Phelps possesses larger-than-average hands (makes for great paddles), a long and broad torso (floatation device anyone?), nearly perfect 50/50 length ratio of upper and lower body, and a relatively small head (less drag and less strain on the neck). In short, Michael Phelps was built to swim. Nature endowed him with these clearly advantageous features. Perhaps not advantageous for a computer programmer—he might need custom keyboards—but certainly for a swimmer.

Nurture is all the encouragement, support, and investments his parents gave during his childhood as well as all the coaching, education, swim meets, and competitions. On top of that, Phelps worked very hard, often training for hours a day. In his biography, he speaks about how nurture enhanced his natural talent:

> In some sports, you can excel if you have natural talent. Not in swimming. You can have all the talent in the world, be built just the right way, but you can't be good or get good without hard work. In swimming, there's a direct connection between what you put in and what you get out of it...

> ...with hard work, with belief, with confidence and trust in yourself and those around you, there are no limits.

All these factors contributed to Phelps' phenomenal career as a pro swimmer, garnering over 28 medals with 23 golds—the most ever won, not just by a swimmer but by *any* Olympic athlete.

Now you might have average hands, a moderately sized head, and you probably haven't won gold medals in swimming like Phelps. But there are natural abilities you *do* have—call them talents. Things you are capable of doing that come more easily to you than to others. Things that you see others struggling with and wonder why. It's just so easy for you, after all.

You might have a facility with words, numbers, patterns, colours, music, or plasticine. Maybe there were subjects you found easier in school—subjects you didn't have to study as hard as others for, you just "got" them and could excel with relatively little effort.

And then there are your hobbies. We tend to get good at our hobbies and interests because we're not under the pressure of earning a living from them. On the contrary, our hobbies are where we tend to *spend* this living, often more so than on our professional development.

These abilities, interests and experiences accumulate to give us a unique set of skills that indicate areas of strength. They are therefore worthy of investigation as candidates for your Vital Few. Working with these strengths is attractive for two main reasons —relative ease and enjoyment.

Ease: Working with what we are good at reduces how much work we must do to create value. In fact, you might have already produced significant value from these abilities. You might even be feeling the tension of wanting more from these skills and "taking things to the next level".

For example, one of the factors that led to me coaching clients in persuasive presentation skills was how relatively easily and intuitively I was able to present. I say relatively because I still had to work hard, however, I got the sense that I wasn't working as hard as many around me, and I was achieving good results.

In terms of nature and nurture, I chock it off to the exposure to being on stage from an early age. Over my formative years, I acted in plays, belonged to an Acapella group, competed in debates, sang in a choir, and even performed in a hip-hop dance group. The fear of public performances was something I had unwittingly overcome. Or, more accurately, never even learned because I started performing too early in my life to become self-conscious.

Because of this, I was ahead of most people who struggled with speaking in public and I knew I could help them. I felt especially drawn to people who were doing well in their fields and otherwise very capable, but who just needed help communicating their value to those who could benefit from it.

What followed was a lot of work studying myself and others, deconstructing what was working and what wasn't, and then distilling it all into a system that delivered results for myself and my clients.

But it began by homing in on something I found myself to be good at—public speaking. You could say that I arrived here, in part, thanks to blind luck. All the hard work of development aside, I certainly didn't join a choir in my early teens with the hopes of one day becoming a corporate coach specializing in persuasive speaking, but here I am.

You too might find the abilities that hold the most value for you aren't the ones you have consciously and intentionally acquired. They might have just happened. And that's ok. Turning them into valuable pieces of your Vital Few may require work, but it will be relatively easy because, well, you are good at them already.

This is the magic of taking the things you are good at seriously. It is a huge labour-saving strategy that puts you in the fast lane. You almost certainly will need the help and support of others and there is, of course, no avoiding work—you will still do a lot of it. But much less than you would have to do if you were working on something that's not a strength. Overall, the positive upshot of working in your strength is that given the same amount of work, you will derive a lot more value than working in your weakness.

Enjoyment: Another fortunate consequence of working on our strength is that things we are good at—especially those we got good at free of financial, professional, or social pressures—are usually things we enjoy. Otherwise, why would we spend our cash and precious time on them? The upshot is that because we enjoy them, we are more likely to spend time getting even better at them. Combine this with our inherent abilities and advantages in these areas and what we have is a potentially game-changing suite of skills.

Create a good@ list

For the reasons we have seen so far, the question "What am I good at?" is a pregnant one with the potential to deliver a big piece of your Vital Few. That's why I invite you to create what I call your good@ list. All you need is a pen and a sheet of paper.

Take as much time as you need right now and make a bullet list of things you are good at. If you're struggling to come up with points, you can use the prompts below:

- Subjects I understand easily
- Hobbies I have
- Things people compliment me on
- Things I just do easily
- Things I'm just better at than most people
- Activities I enjoy (even if they are not hobbies)
- What I spend most of my disposable income on
- Clubs I belong to
- Where I volunteer my time
- Sports I play
- Things I collect

Now re-read and reflect on your list. You might start to see a pattern, you might not. But going through this exercise will give you insight into aspects of yourself you hadn't considered seriously before. And perhaps, more importantly, it will start to give you a hint at potential aspects of your Vital Few.

You don't have to become a professional in all these areas. In fact, some things are best left as hobbies we use only for play; we do need to rest and relax with something we enjoy, don't we? But this exercise will show you how much you could be doing, how many interests and abilities you have that you've never seriously thought about.

You may find that you're working the hardest, perhaps even building your career, in areas where your interests or abilities are middling, to the exclusion of areas where you could be truly great. Interestingly, it might also reveal to you how much your attention is skewed in the direction of activities and pursuits for which you care very little.

This exercise might also prove troubling for two possible reasons.

Firstly, you might feel your list is the wrong length—either too long or too short. In reality, it is unique to you so it being "too" anything doesn't really come into it. It just *is*. That said, if you think it's too short, realize that this will make it easier for you since the goal is not to stroke the ego but to arrive at a Vital *Few* things to develop. If, on the other hand, you have a laundry list of things you are good at and you feel confused, look for patterns and themes and go from there. Later in this chapter, you will see how you can narrow this down using the Vital Venn.

Secondly, it might be distressing if you find a large gap between your abilities and interests and what you find yourself doing the most, or maybe even how you earn your living. Don't fret. There are more questions to come to help you clarify. In the meantime, let this insight *excite* you, not scare or sadden you. You have gained powerful knowledge that can help you design a more fulfilling life for yourself.

Yes, changing directions can be hard and there are various internal and external hurdles to overcome. But with some wisdom and planning, you can begin to move in the new direction with no whiplash.

Before we go on, let us briefly address a force that could undo all the benefits this exercise provides—your ego.

It's important to understand what the ego is, its value, and the purpose it serves. The ego, or *ID*, is the self that seeks preservation, the self that identifies as separate from other people. As valuable as it is, however, it does have drawbacks and can become a source of stumbling. For instance, after studying your list, you may find that what you're good at is not what you have been working hard at. This could feel like a blow to your ego. You might also find you're not good at some things that you wish you were; say you're a person who prides yourself on technical ability, and you find after reflecting that you owe your success to your ability to relate to people more so than your technical skills. This could bruise your ego and so the tendency is to reject the notion.

Recognize that this is the ego speaking. It's more concerned with saving face than it is with your advancement—it's more interested in preservation than progress.

When doing the exercise, be brutally honest with yourself. You will gain so much by shushing this selfish part of yourself on your march to better and more excellent things. As you explore your Vital Few as an individual, always beware of the ego.

What are we good at? A vital question for organizations

For organizations, the question of what you are good at will look different. Organizations don't have large hands to make them better swimmers. But just like individuals, organizations have certain abilities and things they do better than other organizations. And just like individuals, exploring how these can be used to generate or increase value for the customer and the organization is a worthwhile exercise.

In fact, an organization can get so good at something that they become extremely valuable in the eyes of other organizations, leading to profitable mergers and acquisitions. Facebook's acquisitions of WhatsApp and Instagram and Amazon's assimilation of robotics companies Kiva and Canvas are noteworthy examples of this. These were all record-breaking acquisitions; Amazon bought Kiva in 2012 for a whopping $770 million and Facebook bought Instagram for an eye-crossing $1 billion.

These deals could happen because the companies had become extremely good at doing something that the larger organization wanted to start doing. Instead of trying to get good at something new, the larger organizations simply bought a company that was already good at it.

Even if your organization's goal isn't to be bought out by a big company, gaining clarity on the organization's strengths is useful for developing a strategy. For small and medium businesses, it can inform what niche the organization centers on. Instead of trying to play in every field, the company can pitch its tent in a corner of the field and cultivate it intelligently.

Simply put, finding out what your organization is good at is an indication of what game you should play. And like any game, the better you are at it, the better your chances of winning. A good example of this is the Calgary-based data consulting firm Groundswell Group.

An important seed

Groundswell Group was started in 2001 with a staff of two—Cofounders Darren Sartison and Morgan Arndt—and three contractors operating from a tiny office in Calgary. Today, the company employs 200 full-time staff (mostly consisting of highly-specialized data consultants) and has expanded to three offices in Calgary, Vancouver, and Edmonton.

But it's not this growth of 2 to 200 that I found impressive—it's the fact that despite numerous ups and downs in the local and global economy over two decades, Groundswell Group has had only one year where profits did not grow. Every other year it has grown consistently in revenue and profits by an average of 12.5%. Even in that one year—the infamous "flat year" as it is referred to within the company—the company didn't make a loss, it simply maintained its position.

My first contact with Groundswell took place when I was brought on board as a coach and consultant to help the company's highly-technical consultants develop and deliver compelling value propositions and improve their overall communication skills. During the six-week program—which involved travelling to Groundswell's locations and meeting with the company's highly talented consultants—I met with the President of the company, cofounder Darren Sartison.

Standing at 6ft 3, Darren is hard to miss in a room. He looked more like an NFL quarterback than a CEO of a tech company. But not in an intimidating, I'll kick your butt on the field any day kind of way, it was more of a calm presence and friendliness.

Getting a sense of just how unique this company was, I couldn't help but ask Darren what the secret was for Groundswell's success? How was it that such a relatively small company could be competing with massive multi-national companies...and *winning?*

Darren smiled from across the white coffee table in the sleekly designed lunch space of the Calgary downtown office and said to me, "You know, I believe it's because right from the start, we were as clear about what Groundswell is *not* as much as we were about what Groundswell *is*." He went on, "There were times even while we were young and growing and needing business that we were tempted to do many different things. But we knew what we were good at and what we wanted to be known for. And I think that has made all the difference in the unique position we hold today."

We chatted some more about the strategic aspects of the project I was working on, and then we both said goodbye and got back to work.

It would be another two years before I put pen to paper to create this book on the Vital Few. And while this book is a culmination of many different studies, conversations, and experiences, that interaction with Groundswell's president, was an important seed. So naturally, when the time came to write this book, I reached out to Darren for a chat again. This time, I really wanted to get to the root of what he said in our previous meeting.

How to get a groundswell

Our second meeting happened in Darren's office. By now the company had moved to a larger space still in Downtown Calgary. All while the economy in Calgary was going through a downturn.

I wanted to get to the heart of how Groundswell applied the principle of the Vital Few, even if they didn't call it that. When I asked Darren how important focus was to the success of the business, he told me that it pretty much defined the company.

But hey, focus is trending. I wanted some real examples of how the company's focus had paid off. So, Darren told me a story.

A few years prior, he got a call from the Chief Information Officer (CIO) of one of the largest heavy machinery distributing companies in the world. They had heard of Groundswell's expertise and were considering doing business with them. I knew enough to know that Chief Executives of multi-national companies of this magnitude do not call companies to initiate business. Instead, companies lobby and push hard to get an opportunity to make proposals. And then they lobby some more and hope to get picked.

"So, your focus made you stand out from the crowd?" I asked.

"Yes, but there's more."

Darren told me the story of how he had flown over to meet with the company CIO and in the meeting, his host did an interesting thing. After welcoming the Groundswell President into his office and exchanging pleasantries, he handed him a letter-sized card. On it, in bold font and classic corporate poster-style were the company's twelve strategic goals for the year.

"We need help with these goals. Can Groundswell help us?"

The Groundswell president studied the card for a few seconds. Then he placed it on the table where both he and the CIO could see it. He then pointed to two of the twelve, "That one. And that one."

The CIO smiled, "That! Is the right answer."

Darren explained to me that it wasn't the right answer because the CIO had pre-determined what he wanted Groundswell to do for the company. It was the right answer because it showed focus. The executive had been impressed that where other companies might have made grand claims of being able to help with a lot more or even all twelve goals, Groundswell had only picked two.

The focus and clarity impressed the CIO so much that it led to a long and mutually beneficial relationship that spanned many years. I guess you could call those the Vital Two that made all the difference.

This story was an example of how being focused on a vital few areas led to a payoff for the company. But I also wanted to know if Groundswell had passed up any potential business in staying true to this philosophy.

Darren shared a story of how a few of the company's consultants had approached him with some intel. One of the largest telecommunications companies in Canada at the time was a client. The consultants had learnt that the client was making moves to revamp its customer relationship management (CRM) software and process. The consultants saw this as an opportunity for Groundswell and so they spoke to their leadership about it.

As Darren shared this story, I could see the pride he had in his team for being as engaged as they were and watching out for the company.

"So, did you do it?" I asked him.

"We don't do CRM." Darren said plainly, "We just are not set up for it. And setting up for it would take a lot of time and effort and also take us away from doing what we do best."

"So, what happened?" I asked.

"One of our competitors got it. And did quite well I believe. And that's ok."

"Do you *ever* go outside your focus?"

"In an industry like ours, it's important to stay current and ahead of the curve. We try to identify trends and position ourselves in light of our strengths. So our focus may shift based on what is happening around us—new technologies and vendors or more disruptive developments like the move to Cloud-based data management for example." He went on, "We watch for these developments and decide where we want to fit. Once we have that, we put all we've got behind it and try not to get distracted."

I thanked him for his time, but before leaving I asked him if there was anything he wanted to share with someone who would be reading this book. He mentioned two things.

First, he said it's important to have systems and processes set up and optimized to make it easier for you to work within your area of focus. That way, when the opportunity arises, you can mobilize quickly and deliver effectively. This applies whether you are an individual or a large company.

And second, he explained that Groundswell has grown and been successful because of its people, focus, and strategy. As people and companies grow, it's easy to forget this. But as we grow, strategy becomes *more* not less important.

2. WHAT IS WORKING ALREADY?

The question of what is working already is easily overlooked, yet it's a potential Occam's Razor to cut through the clutter to the center of your Vital Few. On the surface the question appears simple, but how often do you ask it?

Businesses benefit from focusing on products and services that are already doing well. It's good to thoughtfully expand, but not at the detriment of a thriving aspect of the business—whether that be a specific product or service or a segment of the market or client-base. Seeking to understand and better serve in these profitability sweet spots will yield better profit-to-expense ratios. In part, because the client-base already exists, but also because the company already has the infrastructure, talent, and resources in place to deliver—as opposed to having to create or heavily revamp its operations to accommodate a new offering.

Sometimes, what's working well for a company is not something the company has invested time and resources developing. It might be a process or technology they stumbled upon and really benefited from but simply lack the infrastructure or human resources they need to maintain it. Other times, it might be a market segment or client need that is proving very profitable but for which they have not earmarked resources for.

Whatever the case, the company has dabbled, struck gold, and now, knowing this approach is working, have found a piece of their Vital Few. The thing to do then is seriously investigate the possibility of doing *more* of that thing. There are often creative ways to pivot if leaders in organizations are willing to do so.

But it's not just companies who can benefit from asking this easy question—you can too. As I did when I was trying to get more clients and grow my business. I simply asked, where did the clients I currently have come from? In other words, what is already working?

A little digging revealed that my clients were coming from two major sources—my blog and my speaking engagements. That is, people who had found my content online, liked it and wanted to work personally with me, and people who had heard me speak at an event and wanted to dig deeper into the content I shared or bring me in to work with their organizations. Once this was clear, the next step was obvious—do more of what was already working.

So, I spent more of my time creating useful articles for my blog. I also spent more time developing seminars and talks that I could deliver to companies. Not only did this increase my revenue from speaking but it also converted more audience members into coaching clients.

These two seemingly simple changes led to a doubling of my revenue in just one year. I even had to stop taking on clients at one point—a decision that was hard but necessary—to make time to provide good service to the clients I already had at the time. And it all came about by simply identifying what was working, and then doing more of it.

Zeroing in on what was working helped me achieve more by doing less. The quality of my work could improve because I was focused. And because I was working in a space that was already yielding good results, I could be confident in my efforts. Also, since I was working in familiar territory, I didn't have to do anything new and unwonted. I could just invest my resources in what was already there.

So, what is already working for you? What are you doing (or have done) that has produced the results you wanted? Got it? Now do more of it. It's that easy. At least in principle. The practice of it is not always so clear-cut, especially with so many competing priorities. Yet that is what we have been talking about so far—*something* has to give so you can get more out of your efforts.

Sometimes what you discover is working is something you enjoy and are good at. In this case, it's easy to do more of it; like my public speaking bringing in more business. But you might also find that what is already working is not what you necessarily enjoy or are particularly good at. As long as the goal it helps you reach is a worthy one for you, then the decision needs to be made whether it's worth the time to learn it for yourself or to delegate it to someone who is good at it (this is covered in detail in chapter 5).

Similar to working in your strength, the approach of doing more of what is working is often easier than trying something completely new. In fact, always chasing after "new" at the expense of what is working can be actively *counterproductive*. This shiny object syndrome doesn't let us stick with anything long enough to give it a chance to produce results. Instead, it makes us jump from one new thing to another, never really maturing in anything.

Now I'm not saying that you should *never* try something new. In fact, you likely found the things that work today by trying something new and realizing that it works. What I am saying is that you don't need a lot of new things working for you to be successful. You need a Vital Few working at their best to produce most of your results. And sometimes the clue to those Vital Few are in the things that are working already. All you may need to do is fine-tune or otherwise optimize them to get even better results.

The act of finding what is already working is, therefore, an important one. That said, sometimes what is already working might not be the answer. Maybe because the environment is changing and you foresee that what is working now is at risk of failing in the near future. That is, what worked before may not continue to work for much longer.

In this situation, the worst thing to do is stubbornly persist or bury your head in the sand. Denial of this kind is fatal. The tyrannical attachment to the cliché of "this is how we have always done it" has laid many low.

It's important to realize that things change, the landscape changes, and you must adapt. This is when you must ask the incisive question: Where is my value?

3. WHERE IS MY VALUE?

Value is so central to our lives that without it, we would be unable to act. Everything we do is driven by value and our core values drive us.

Understanding not just what we value but how much we value it is important in determining our Vital Few. This is because our values can unlock a treasure trove of motivation.

A person who values money highly can be motivated by it. Such a person will be more driven to pursue activities that add to their sense of material abundance. Someone else who values prestige may instead be motivated by recognition such as a company or association award even if (perhaps *because*) there is no cash prize associated. For both these people and for you, the question of values is an important one.

It's difficult to press forward in the face of challenges if we are pressing after something we don't consider worthwhile. Answering the question of what we value will unlock drive, creativity, energy, ingenuity, and perseverance—qualities we need to attain and maintain success.

But this is still only part of the equation. To zoom in on our Vital Few through the lens of value, we must ask another question: what does our audience value? I use the word "audience" here loosely. I could have easily used client, customer, company, boss, teammate, or even family. Feel free to insert any of these.

What our audience values is almost more important than what we value as far as being effective in our use of TVF. I know this might sound like a contradiction given the earlier discussion on the importance of our own values, but it isn't. If you find yourself in the service of an audience whose values are diametrically opposite to yours, you are serving the wrong audience. And you will always struggle.

In fact, when your values are clearly defined, they will help you define your audience. Few things will cause frustration with as much reliability as trying to serve the wrong audience. So, as much as it is important to understand your values, it's just as important to understand what your audience values, and then to work at the point where both converge. Or to seek out a different audience.

They sold seashells by the shore

In the early 19th century, the company we know today as the oil and gas giant Shell was an antique store that sold actual seashells in London. During that period, the demand for seashells in the interior decoration industry was so high that the company's founder, Marcus Samuel, built a profitable business importing them from the Far East.

At the time, intercontinental trade relied on sea-travel and Samuel's company utilized this channel greatly in their business. This led to the company developing a strong import-export system that went on to become an import-export business in its own right. In fact, by 1897, the company was renamed by the founder's sons and heirs of the business to the Shell Transport and Trading Company.

It was the system of trade itself and not the seashells that proved to be what was valuable. It was what positioned the company to take advantage of the burgeoning oil industry which was picking up pace as a viable replacement to coal as a source of energy at the time. And as the company invested and innovated in shipping, it rode the waves to become the successful energy company it is today.

But it all stemmed from recognising that their value was in their systems of trade, *not* what they traded. The company has, however, kept to their roots by maintaining the shell as their visual identity, perhaps because it's easier to draw than a cargo ship or a flowchart.

The Shell story is instructive to companies and individuals alike. It is on us to find out the true source of value in the work we do in order to keep our work valuable.

THE VITAL VENN

The intersection of the three questions discussed in this chapter will point us strongly and emphatically to where we should be focusing our energies. When we find that zone where what we are good at coincides with where the value lies and what is working already, we hit paydirt.

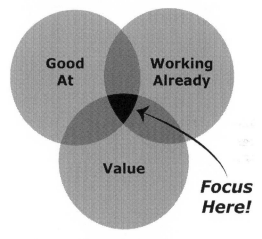

Figure: The Vital Venn

CHAPTER 4

The Trivial Many

The Trivial Many is the antithesis to the vital few. We can't talk about the Law of the Vital Few without looking at the dark side of the Trivial Many. It would be like talking about Yin but never mentioning Yang; like talking about Jekyl but neglecting Hyde; like Skywalker without Vader...you get the picture.

To understand the Trivial Many, let's re-visit the 80/20 Principle. Remember from Chapter 1 that the 80/20 principle says that 80% of our outputs come from 20% of our efforts. That's straightforward enough—find that 20% and you have identified your Vital Few. But wait, you've only accounted for 20% of your efforts, what's going on with the remaining 80%? It is this 80% of efforts that produce a paltry 20% of results that constitute the Trivial Many.

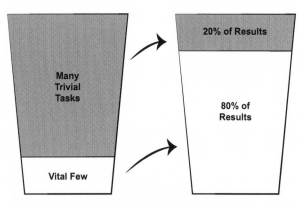

Figure: The Vital Few and The Trivial Many

The Trivial Many are the numerous activities we engage in that take up the bulk of our energy and resources but return only very few results. I am all too familiar with this phenomenon; let me share a story from my life that rather painfully illustrates this.

A DANGEROUS WORK EXPERIMENT

I once had a job where one of my responsibilities was to create a weekly report—the kind that turned data into information for decisions, as they say. The report took about three to four hours to create and every week without fail, I would put it together. I didn't really enjoy doing it and, if I'm being honest, I knew I could do more and wanted to. But I also knew that companies don't promote people who suck at their jobs. This report was a part of my job, just like it had been for the guy before me. So, I did my best at it.

Tedious as it was, it was all worth it when, on Friday afternoon, I would finish the document, open up my email, populate the recipient field with some pretty important names in the company, lean back, and ever so proudly click send. Every few weeks, I'd get a thank you email back saying that the report had been very useful and helped with an important decision. *Insert proud self-pat on the back here*

And then one week, things got busy. So busy, the unthinkable happened—I forgot to send the report.

"That's it!" I thought on Monday, "That's it! There goes my job, my paycheck and my prospects! I'm going to get fired and have to spend hours in resume clinics salvaging my career and hours in counselling salvaging my self-esteem! This is it! This is how it ends!"

Well, Monday rolled around and…nothing. Then Tuesday… nothing. By Wednesday, I should have started working on the present week's report, but mischievous curiosity won over common sensibility.

"I wonder…" I thought, "What would happen if I didn't send the report for two weeks in a row?" Only one way to find out.

Nothing happened. Three weeks? Nothing. For four weeks straight, no report and for four weeks straight, nothing happened. By week five, on the verge of a tension-triggered heart attack, I decided to end the dangerous experiment and send the report. Four hours later, I had put it together as usual, sent it off and breathed a sigh of relief. And, true to form, nothing happened.

That one-month dance with death got me thinking—how important was this report? I decided to get some answers.

One afternoon not long after, I was in a meeting with a department head, Kyle, and I asked him about the report and how it was being used.

"Oh, Anthony!" Kyle said, coffee-cup in hand, "Those reports are invaluable during our quarterly meetings."

Wait. Did he just say *quarterly* meetings?

He continued, "It's really great to have the most up-to-date numbers available when we need them."

No wonder I got the thank you emails every few weeks— that was when they were actually using the report. I was sending reports four times a month when they were only needed four times a year!

This tedious, soul-sucking, low-return-giving activity belonged in the Trivial Many hall of fame. I promptly adjusted and with the time and space I created, I was able to work on a process improvement project that led to a promotion within the organization.

That experience has made me acutely aware and rather mercenary about quickly determining how much value different aspects of my work life produce.

If you begin to look closely, you too will find numerous instances of things you're doing that are adding very little, if any, value to you. Sometimes, like the report from my experiment, they are things that need doing but maybe don't need *so much* doing.

In other cases, they are things we have no business doing at all, or we're just not the best person to do them.

THE CASE OF KB

Take the case of one client who we will call KB. He and I worked together following his promotion to a senior management position with one of the largest retailers in Canada. Prior to this, he had been a mid-level manager with the company, but he quickly stood out for his stellar performance. So, naturally, when there was an opening in a senior role, he was pegged.

But with a new role came new challenges. His promotion required more sophisticated communication skills and more strategic leadership. But KB was up for it, so he reached out and we got to work.

We initially focused on his presence and presentation skills. And it was during one of our sessions practising some influential communication skills that it became evident that things were not quite right with how KB was allocating his efforts. After listening to a section of an important update he was planning to give to the managers now reporting to him, I remarked, "This table shows a lot of numbers. It will be more effective to focus on what the numbers mean."

"Sure, I'll fix that."

"Ok. Also, the colours seem washed out. It's minor, but your team may not be able to see this clearly and the impact will be lost."

"Ok. I'll work on those later too."

"Hang on. Are *you* doing all this work yourself?"

"Of course. I always have."

"I see… let's talk about that for a bit."

I discovered that KB had been doing a lot of his old activities himself, down to compiling his division's numbers and designing all his presentation slides. He even compiled the numbers for the team's performance each week.

Doing this work might have made sense in his previous position, but in this new position these activities—as valuable and important as they were—had moved into the Trivial Many. To make matters worse, these activities were taking time away from what he could be doing—the work of strategic leadership that had highlighted him for the promotion in the first place.

KB is talented and hardworking, but his efforts were being sapped with the tedium of spreadsheets and presentation slides, among other things. It made more sense for him to delegate that activity to someone who could do it faster and better. Then he could simply review and make changes if needed.

We implemented that and with more focus on the vision for his division and leveraging some of the work on influential communication, KB was able to plot a course for his division and garner the buy-in of his team. One of the managers who reported to him even remarked that he found KB's foresight inspiring—which probably wouldn't have happened if he had been too busy hunting for fonts or chart templates.

KB is a good example of what a lot of us do. We mistake the fact that something needs doing to mean that we need to be doing it. The old adage "if you want something done right, do it yourself" is patently false. If I want my car brakes done right, I better *not* do it myself. The same goes for many other things in life. There are people skilled at things we suck at, so why wouldn't we leverage their abilities? Our Trivial Many falls into the Vital Few for a lot of people. And while we toil and sweat, taking hours to get these things done, time (and life) pass us by.

NOT WORTH THE SQUEEZE

One of the hallmarks of Trivial Many activities is that they add so little value compared to the effort they gobble up that the juice is not worth the squeeze. These no-juice-giving, finger-numbing acts take way more than they give back. They can be work activities that keep us busy but add no value whatsoever, or relationships that are high-maintenance but low return—or worse—parasitic.

From an organizational perspective, many companies are gung-ho about adopting new processes but bashful when it comes to purging the relics of old ones. These time-consuming and tedious processes continue to be perpetuated until someone comes along and starts asking some basic questions like, "Why are we doing this?" To which the answer often is, "Well, we always have."

This is what happened in my case with the infamous weekly report. There was a time when the organization *needed* to increase the frequency of those reports to tide management through a tight budget period. During that crisis, it made sense to keep a closer eye on the numbers. But then, once the storm was over, the process persisted and was perpetuated until someone came along and asked the basic question, "Why?"

Organizations should purge as much as they purchase. In fact, companies should adopt a principle of finite space in which new processes are not introduced without consideration for what that process will make redundant or unnecessary. Get into the habit of asking the basic question, "Why are we doing this?"

Similarly, in your personal life, there may be relics from times past that are eating up your time and resources. They may be excessive time spent in leisure, old friendships you have outgrown but continue to toil over, or just ways of doing things or spending your time that you could make more beneficial for yourself.

Time for some action to get you started. This week, notice any activities you engage in that take 20 minutes or more and ask yourself these four questions:

- Why am I doing this?
- What am I benefitting from this?
- Could I be doing something more beneficial?
- Is there a more efficient way to do this?

With the answers to these four questions, you should be able to quickly assess whether the activity belongs in your Vital Few or your Trivial Many. Take special note if these are activities you perform often or routinely because that means you are spending a lot more time on them in the long-run.

Why 20 minutes? Well, this is the functional unit of time in which worthwhile work can be accomplished. Some activities will take longer, others less, but if you spend 20 minutes of concentrated effort on something, you'll likely make good progress. Even 20 minutes of deep and intentional rest and relaxation can work wonders. Whatever deserves 20 minutes of your time better be providing some benefit in return.

The bare necessities

If you deem an activity unnecessary, then the answer is manifest—stop it. Period. Or at least begin the process of stopping it. Spend less and less time doing it until you eradicate the habit.

Sometimes though an activity is not necessary, but we still derive value from it. An example might be watching TV. It's not necessary, but it might provide us with some entertainment and help us unwind. For activities like these, the thing to do is *minimize* them. Take some time from them to give to higher-value activities.

The main point to takeaway here is that you can take one of three approaches to the Trivial Many in your life—delegate, eliminate or minimize. For the necessary, delegate them to an efficient and competent person or system to free you up for more high-value activities. And for the unnecessary, your first option is to eliminate them. If that is not possible, then at least minimize them.

The next chapter provides a straightforward model to help make this decision easier.

CHAPTER 5

Value, Effort and the TVF Matrix

Knowing that some activities are part of our Vital Few and others are part of the Trivial Many is one thing. But it's not always easy to determine which is which. In other words, what activities give you the most return on your invested time and lifeforce and which ones are just not worth the squeeze?

You don't want to assume something is trivial and stop doing it only to find out it was actually very important. On the other hand, you don't want to keep doing something if it's not providing much return. And even if you were able to determine where your activities go—TVF or Trivial Many—what do you do with each pile?

It's because of these tricky questions that I created the TVF Matrix. And, keeping true to the spirit of doing more by doing less, the matrix pivots on two critical hinges—value and effort. The TVF Matrix contains two zones made up of two quadrants each for a total of four quadrants. Let's step through each one and talk about what to do with the activities that fall into them.

THE ZONE OF DRAIN

The zone of drain is the lower half of the TVF Matrix —the plane of *low value*. And because of that, activities that fall into this zone have the effect of sapping energy but not providing much return.

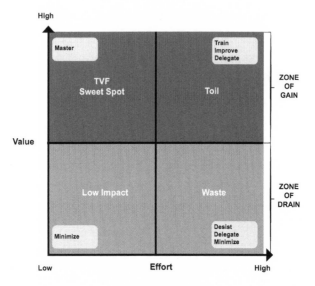

Figure: The TVF Matrix

The Quadrant of Low Impact: Low Effort/Low Value (LELV)

This quadrant is home to activities (LELV activities) that take very little effort but also offer or produce very little value. Leisure activities typically fall in this quadrant. But they are not the only things that belong here because not everything that falls in this quadrant is necessarily enjoyable.

For example, watching TV for entertainment is low effort and low value but probably enjoyable. However, if you are like me, loading up and running the dishwasher, though low impact and low effort, is not particularly fun.

In short, *any* activity that is not strenuous but also not particularly productive for you based on your personal and professional goals falls into this quadrant.

What to do with the Quadrant of Low Impact

Minimize LELV activities as much as possible. Leisure has its place and it's not realistic to assume that everything we do will provide or produce huge value—this would put us under immense self-afflicted pressure. You can remain very effective while getting away with some LELV. Just aim to keep them to a manageable minimum. Besides, since the effort expenditure is small, this quadrant is not as bad as it initially seems. It is its neighbour we must avoid like the plague—the quadrant of waste.

The Quadrant of Waste: High Effort/Low Value (HELV)

This is the second quadrant in the Zone of Drain. Activities that fall in this zone (HELV activities) are characterized by demanding a lot of effort but providing little value. They leave you exhausted but not much better off. Right away you see that this is the quadrant you want to avoid the most.

You have already read a classic example of this in my dangerous work experiment from chapter 4. The report I so dutifully and painstakingly completed, though costing high effort on my part, was providing low value to me and the organization in comparison. There might be similar HELV activities living rent-free in your life too.

Our human tendency is to think that effort expended is proportional to output. That is, activities that take time and effort to complete *must* be commensurately valuable. As we have seen with TVF, this is a fallacy. Never assume. Take a very close look at the activities you are performing that demand considerable effort to confirm how much value they are *really* producing.

This is not always easy to do, especially where those activities are part of a job description. However, if upon investigation you find that a considerable number of your activities fall in this quadrant of waste, a revamp is in order. And when you do the revamp, be ruthless.

What to do with the Quadrant of Waste

The most direct response to activities in this quadrant is to cease and desist with immediate effect. Why continue to expend precious stores of life-force on an activity that is not giving anything valuable back? This is the first and most decisive response to the discovery of these productivity saboteurs—chuck them overboard.

But tempting as this may be, recall the question of necessity explored previously. What makes this quadrant dangerous is not the low value part of the equation, but the *combination* of high effort and low value.

To deal with the tricky situation where the activities that fall in this quadrant for you are still required, remember, a quadrant of waste for you might be a quadrant of low impact or even a TVF Sweet Spot for another better-suited agent.

Therefore, the second approach you can take is to delegate your HELV activities to others who will not be as negatively impacted and might even enjoy themselves.

For example, I recently delegated the activity of vacuuming to a robot—a much more capable agent. Does the robot enjoy it? I doubt it. But it sure does it better than I do and can reach places I cannot. Best of all, it can work while I sleep or read. The time and effort saved has paid back many times over.

There might be activities you can also delegate to move you out of the HELV quadrant. As suggested in the Vital Venn chapter, organizations should revisit their workflows to expose areas that can be improved. Over time, business operations can come to reside with departments or individuals that have to work extra hard to fulfil them due to administrative bottlenecks and convoluted channels of communication. This happens more from neglect than malicious intent as pockets of work that depend on each other change without a big picture review of the impacts of those changes.

Reviewing and modifying the workflows to ensure that the least viable effort is expended will not only improve organizational productivity, it will also have a huge positive impact on employee morale since work will be organized to minimize any HELV work, if only by moving into the LELV quadrant of the same (or other) person or team.

The third and, to my mind, *least* desirable option is to minimize these HELV activities. It is not always possible to completely eliminate these activities, though that is the ideal we ought to strive for. Sometimes, we are simply not in a position to stop performing these time-wasting activities instantly—maybe we have discovered them and even presented them to our bosses or boards, but these parties are playing catch up. In the meantime, things need doing and life is being lived.

Furthermore, delegation may not be possible due to constraints of finding the finances or talent (or robot) to perform the activity. In all these cases, the best we can do is minimize the activity. Find out the *least* amount of it you can get away with, and then do no more than that—all the while harbouring the goal of eliminating it the minute you can.

THE ZONE OF GAIN

The zone of gain is in the upper half of the TVF Matrix. This zone sits in the plane of *high value*. And because of this high value, activities that fall into this zone are worthy of close consideration.

The Quadrant of Toil: High Effort/High Value (HEHV)

Toil (Verb): To work extremely hard and incessantly. To move slowly and with difficulty. (Noun): Long strenuous fatiguing labour

Activities that fall into this quadrant (HEHV activities) are those that provide important benefits to us but require a great deal of work and strain on our part. These activities tend to require skill to perform—skills we do not possess or possess at a level too low to make us efficient at them.

An example that comes to mind is tax accounting. Everyone, whether businesspeople or employees, can benefit greatly from a smart tax strategy as part of their wealth-building plan. But tax laws in most countries are not easy to decipher. In fact, a quick read of a country's tax code will lead to the suspicion that it's almost like the writers *don't want* you to be able to understand it. The consequences of breaking tax laws are serious yet there are benefits embedded in the jargon that also go unnoticed. It therefore makes a lot of sense to use a professional once your tax situation gets complicated enough to warrant one.

Yet, many people spend hours and hours calculating their taxes themselves. They may manage to complete it after many hours and web searches, but this is *toil*.

I remember one year while still in university spending many hours over the course of three weeks calculating and filing my taxes. The next year, I employed a professional. With one single deduction that he was able to spot because he was trained, he saved me more than he cost. And then some. It also took a fraction of the time.

Most companies know to use the services of professionals for maintaining their books. Yet there might be other areas in which the company is expending resources in the quadrant of toil—either by hampering the productivity of staff by saddling them with work beyond their skills or continuing to operate divisions of the business that, though profitable to some degree, put strain on the company in tangible as well as intangible ways.

At the end of the day, any activity that produces benefit but also demands high effort expenditure falls into the quadrant of toil.

What to do with the Quadrant of toil

This quadrant of toil is a tricky one for most. Because it provides significant value, it is easy to justify the time and energy spent. We unconsciously reason that sure, we may have spent ten times as long as a trained agent would have, but we got the rewards, so it's all good.

There is also a somewhat darker psychological ploy at play here—the belief that any benefit that *doesn't* cost a lot of effort is somehow tainted. This defeating belief announces itself deceptively as a "good work ethic". But really, it's a perversion of a good work ethic.

A good work ethic means doing smart work that's efficient and of high quality. This requires us to reconsider the activities in this quadrant and decide how we want to adapt. I offer two suggestions:

1. Delegate/Employ

Activities in the quadrant of toil are excellent candidates for delegation.

You don't have to be a businessperson to employ labour; every time you pay someone money to do something, you are employing their services, whether it be the neighbour's teenager who clears driveways after a snowy night or your tax accountant. Explore this option seriously and see if the value you get from delegating HEHV activities outweighs the upfront cost.

2. Train

Sometimes, an HEHV activity demands excessive effort simply because of a lack of ability or skills. And even though I have already suggested in the first point that you get someone else to do it, sometimes training yourself or your organization in the skills required for this quadrant can nudge the activities in the direction of your TVF Sweet Spot.

This strategy of training should be applied only after checking if any of the following conditions apply:

- **The time to train to a level of proficiency is relatively short.** If it's going to take you or your organization a long time to train for the activity, consider delegating instead to specialized agents. However, this should be considered in light of the next condition.
- **The long-term benefits of the skill are high.** It might be worth training for skills that have recurring returns over the long term. However, do not train for transient skills, skills that are costly relative to their long-term value, or skills that require high maintenance if they are not intrinsic to your Vital Few.
- **The cost of delegation exceeds the difference in value created**. In other words, training for the skill is less costly than delegating or employing. Keep in mind that cost and value here are more than money. It might cost money to delegate, but the value from delegation can be indirect. On the other hand, there are non-monetary costs associated with having to deal with difficult vendors, agents, or contractors. Revisit this periodically as your career or business grows.

As you can see, the quadrant of toil is painted with nuance. Whereas it is easy to suggest that we do away with the quadrant of waste and shrink the quadrant of low impact, the quadrant of toil calls for deeper deliberation—the kind that makes you want to sit still and ruminate, take a long walk, or journal like crazy. Perhaps even all three in sequence!

But with these guides, you are better equipped to make the right decision for your situation.

The TVF Sweet Spot: Low Effort/High Value (LEHV)

Activities that live in the TVF Sweet Spot provide high value while requiring relatively low effort on your part. They also likely fall in the intersection of your Vital Venn from chapter 3.

What to do with the TVF Sweet Spot

Master and maximize. Concentrating on the LEHV activities will give you the most return on your investment of time and effort. You are probably already reaping disproportionally high benefits from LEHV activities even if you're not aware of it. But you can maximize this return by striving to attain mastery in these areas. Because you already possess abilities in these areas and they have proven to be valuable, you are well-positioned to overcome any hurdles and whiz past the competition.

There is more to come on learning and mastery in Book II—The TVF Disciplines. For now, realize that your TVF Sweet Spot is where you want to concentrate the bulk of your effort because for every unit of effort, the value you create and derive here is greater than any other quadrant in your TVF matrix.

Reflect on these LEHV activities, probe and ponder them. Think about how you can do more of them, and how you can extract the most value from them. Give time and energy to them— at the expense of other activities if necessary. This is your sweet spot, your goldmine—but it must be dug. It is your garden, but it must be cultivated. There is no better time than the present. Like the proverb goes: The best time to plant a tree was 20 years ago; the next best time is now.

Don't be surprised if as you move more of your effort into your TVF Sweet Spot, you find Vital Fews *within* your Vital Few. That is, even within your LEHV quadrant, some activities prove to be even more valuable while needing less strain than others. This is the nature of the law. Exploring, embracing, and engaging this is the path to continuous and never-ending growth and improvement.

To have most of the activities we engage in fall in the TVF Sweet Spot is to have reached the promised land of living the TVF way. It is the ideal to strive for. If more of us spent our time and energy working in our own TVF sweet spot, we would do our best, most beneficial, most enjoyable and most creative work and the world would be a better place for all.

CHAPTER 6

Effecting Change and the Two Yous

I remember having a conversation with a professor of mine in university. I was discussing career prospects with her as I neared the end of grad school. During the conversation, she made a statement that made an impression on me: "You know, Anthony, you are very passionate, and I have no doubt you will do well. In some ways, you remind me of myself. You see, when I started my career, I wanted to change the world. A lot has happened since then. I have learned a lot. Today, I aim to change myself."

Interestingly, she was one of the most respected and decorated faculty members in the department. Her research had influenced many important government policies and she had supervised several graduate students who had gone on to have successful careers. Clearly, she was making a difference and, in fact, changing the world both on a large and smaller, more personal scale. Even though she didn't say it, I suspect the clue to her success lies in the simple but profound shift that happened when she stopped trying to change her environment and instead change herself.

I share this story in an attempt to address a gremlin that might have already crawled into your mind as it did mine when I started taking the ideas of TVF more seriously. Like a brass penny held so close to the eye to block out the golden sun, this gremlin held the changes required to live by the TVF way so close to my face it blocked out the light beyond and made the challenges seem insurmountable. I felt invested in how I was already doing things and was a bit scared to start making the changes this new way of approaching my life seemed to require. Promises of greater benefit and fulfilment aside, I was hesitant to change because I was not sure if I could.

If this is a thought that you are having now, let me just say this —you *can* change.

Something happens as we get older—we become stiff. Not only literally in our muscles—but more importantly, in our thinking. We lose flexibility and it takes conscious effort to stop this from happening; call it staying young at heart or being open-minded. Whatever you call it, in essence, it's choosing flexibility over rigidity.

As you read about this new way of viewing life and work, you might find yourself doubting whether or not it's for you. But this is a gremlin—a self-limiting thought. We hide behind thoughts like these when we are faced with a change that is uncomfortable. We sense the change will be good for us, but because we don't like change, we rationalize it away. We cut off the curiosity the idea sparks because it also bubbles up some atavistic fears.

Sometimes it's because we don't want to do the work. Sometimes, it's because we fear failure. And sometimes it's because we fear success. Human beings, you and I, are weird.

Though this is not a book about overcoming this resistance, acknowledge that you will feel it as you think about the changes that developing TVF in your life will demand. Therefore, it will be helpful to talk about an important aspect of yourself—one you might not have given much thought to, but that the best and enduring thoughts in science and philosophy indicate has a profound impact on how successful you will be at effecting change.

THERE ARE TWO SIDES OF YOU, AT LEAST

This is perhaps the most important concept to grasp in the pursuit of positive change—the fact that most of us are beings in a state of tension. As we will discuss later in chapter 11, one of the things that makes us unique as humans is our ability to think into the future. This creates possibilities as well as challenges.

It means that we can see ourselves as we are now and also see ourselves as we might be in the future. Who we are now may want something that is not so great for who we are in the future. And who we are in the future might benefit from something that who we are today might not enjoy very much.

This creates tension.

It's why we find ourselves acting against our own self-interest and then wondering what went wrong. It's why sometimes we feel like an audience to our own bizarre behaviour.

How often do you find yourself doing something you had resolved not to do all the while being fully aware that you were doing it? Like indulging in an impulse purchase just after drafting a sound budget to help you save or invest more. Or how often do you find yourself in the middle of a sentence that you know will not end well, yet you finish it anyway and then feel awful afterward? People who put their foot in their mouth can usually see it approaching their face but seem powerless to stop it.

Strange as the idea of being a passive audience to our own behaviour might sound, what is perhaps even stranger is the fact that most of the time we are not even alert enough to notice. We are a *sleeping* audience to our own actions. If you have ever tried to recall the details of a routine action like your daily commute or coffee-making and been stumped, then you are experiencing exactly this phenomenon.

It has been described in many metaphors—many of which involve some mix of man and wildlife. From 4th century BC Plato's charioteer and unruly horse to the more modern Tim Urban's rational decision-maker and instant gratification monkey. And in Chip and Dan Heath's excellent book, *Switch*, they borrow a similar metaphor from social psychologist Jonathan Haidt—the rational rider and the emotional elephant.

These metaphors express our dual nature in an insightful and vivid way—the rational, but physically frail thinker (depicted by a human) versus the brawny unruly actor (depicted by wildlife).

The thinker is smart but can't get much done without the actor; the actor is strong but isn't too bright and wants to do its own thing. It also isn't easily persuaded. Success therefore depends on the thinker's intelligence and the actor's energy.

Between thinker and actor, however, is a less-talked-about agency—the one watching the drama unfold. This agency is what I consider the *real* you. Let's call this the Sleepy Decider.

I call it a "decider" because it chooses who gets to call the shots. It is called "sleepy" because, as we have seen already, in most of us it's rarely awake. We live life on autopilot, never exercising our power to observe and even direct the play. Yet it is there and *can* be employed once we start to pay attention to it. When we don't pay attention to it, we submit to the gratification of the moment, giving free rein to the unruly actor, ignoring the thinker jumping up and down and pointing frantically from the sidelines at a bigger, better payoff in the future.

This dynamic of past and future self is perhaps best illustrated through the experiences of another beloved cultural character, Homer. Not the legendary Greek poet Homer (writer of the epic poems *The Iliad* and *The Odyssey*) but the fictional Homer Simpson from the show *The Simpsons* of animated comedy acclaim. This Homer is more known and appreciated for his farcical oafishness and overall ineptitude.

In one episode of the show, he was confronted with the potential consequences of a lifetime of consuming an unhealthy diet. Not wanting to give up his greasy donuts and other decadent treats, Homer declared the iconic words, "That's a problem for future Homer. Man, I don't envy that guy," before defiantly downing a mixture of vodka and mayonnaise and then keeling over in comedic irony.

This "future Homer problem" has become a popular meme for describing behaviours of avoidance, procrastination, and the like.

We all have a present self and a future self. The challenge is balancing the needs of the two. Present self wants to be comfortable and at ease—often at the expense of future self. This is another dimension of the two selves, in this case, separated by time. And again, the Decider must be employed to regulate the relationship between the two to balance the needs of present and future you. Whenever a disconnect occurs between who we are and who we want to become, conflict arises between the two parts of us at play.

Making the shift to living by TVF will trigger this conflict. It will be difficult to eliminate aspects of our lives that have come to feel like a "part of us" but that do not qualify as important enough in terms of TVF. That is, parts of our present self. And it will be challenging to expand previously neglected aspects and even adopt new habits that will become an important part of our future self—the self that lives better because it has come into harmony with your Vital Few.

Keep in mind that the push and pull you feel, that struggle you have within you, those conflicting voices—all of it—is normal.

It's common to all of us, especially those striving to improve themselves. We feel resistance, we flounder sometimes, we have false starts and moments of self-doubt. The thing to do is to recognize when this aspect of ourselves surfaces—and then to adjust and press forward anyway.

It may be difficult to begin with but we humans are amazing at adapting. And this adaptation, though commonly expressed in terms of adapting to negative changes, applies just as patently to positive ones such as striving to live a life according to TVF—a life in which you can have, do, and be more by doing less.

CHAPTER 7

Goals are *Still* Good

Few accomplishments matter, but the ones that matter, matter a lot.

Knowing now where your Vital Few might lie, whether that be the vital few sources of pain and frustration or the vital few levers of success, you are in a good position to set some goals. However, knowing that some goals will provide more returns and make a bigger difference in your life than others, it makes sense to pursue those goals over lesser ones. The more important the problem that the achievement of a goal solves, the higher priority that goal should have. There are many things you *could* be doing. But they are not necessarily what you *should* be doing. What you should be doing is moving in the direction of the high pay-off goals.

Imagine a person going through a rough patch in life. Let's call this person Tracy. Tracy is unemployed, lonely, broke, bored, and depressed. I have personally been each of those things at some point and three all at once (I won't tell you which three, this is about Tracy, not me). Now, Tracy *could* set four different goals—one for each problem. Or Tracy could just set one goal to pretty much cover them all—get a job.

Getting a job would solve the problem of boredom and, by extension, depression as well. Indeed, clinical psychologists have traced strong correlations between depression and unemployment. And, of course, it doesn't take a stretch of the imagination to see how getting a job would help with being unemployed and broke. As for loneliness, being employed might boost Tracey's self-confidence to help her begin socializing again. All in all, a job would be a much more efficient goal to set than, say, creating a dating profile. Not to say that unemployed people should not create dating profiles, but on the scale of priority, perhaps becoming gainfully employed should be higher.

Back to Tracy. After a few weeks of updating resumes, upgrading skills, and attending networking events, Tracy lands a job. With the job comes a renewed sense of pride and confidence, social interactions with adults, a sense of purpose, structure of day-to-day activities, money to spend and spare, heck, maybe even a gym membership! The single goal of getting gainful employment has all but transformed Tracy's life.

This is a simplistic example, I'll admit, and everyone's life is different. But the example is intended to make the point that there can be simpler approaches to solving seemingly complicated, multi-faceted problems. You do not always need a discrete solution for every facet—you might just need to set a bigger, all-encompassing goal. And even though these goals are "bigger", attaining them may not take as much effort as you might initially think. Often, you can *save* energy by focusing on a clear goal and letting the goal direct your activities, rather than scattering your forces trying to address each off-kilter detail.

Like a mechanism made up of many gears, some gears move more weight than others. Some goals move heavy loads and some only lift tiny weights.

THE BIG GOAL SYSTEM

It's not always clear what our next focus—our big goal—should be. Our vision is coloured by our emotions and our views are obscured by urgency. Things that produce or carry a heavy emotional charge for us or things that are immediately apparent to us tend to take up more attention than others. The result is that we may erroneously weigh these things higher when we are trying to decide on what goals to pursue.

Going back to Tracy. If Tracy was scrolling through Facebook where there were posts of friends and their partners frolicking through bucolic scenes set to the background of violin music, well, Tracy might feel pretty low. Driven by the high emotional charge related to it, Tracy might actually want to set the search for a romantic relationship as the most important goal. I want *that*.

But is that really the right goal? Maybe. Maybe not. Likely not. But how could you tell for sure? Or at the very least, how do you help yourself remove the biases that may be clouding your vision? How do stop yourself from spinning out of control?

That is where my Big Goal System (BGS) comes in. The system not only eliminates the tendency for us to set hasty, ill-advised goals, it also helps us stop spinning our wheels and procrastinating on deciding our goals.

We spin our wheels for different reasons. If you are an analytical type, you might spin as you burrow into deep rabbit holes of problem determination, employing complicated models and processes to decide what to work on. If you are a free-spirited type, you might simply freeze due to the overwhelming number of possible goals to pursue, struggling to make wholistic sense of it all.

The BGS cuts through all that and lets you go straight to the point of greatest potential. There are no overly complicated considerations. All that matters are your own experience and your own desires; your own pain and your own potential. You. As you stand now.

That is immensely freeing because once you have completed the BGS, you can decide right away on your own Big Goal. And because it will be yours, not someone else's, you will be 100% responsible for it.

In keeping with TVF, The Big Goal System helps you choose your goals in terms of the Vital Few that will have the most positive impact on your life by drawing on the Wheel of Life framework. This framework was developed by Paul J Meyer and it expresses life in terms of eight segments on a wheel.

Over time, the wheel's categories have been renamed and revamped by different people, but the spirit of the framework can be represented in these eight segments:

1. Health and Fitness
2. Money and Finances
3. Career or Business
4. Social Life
5. Family
6. Personal Growth and Development
7. Hobbies and Recreation (Fun)
8. Spiritual Development

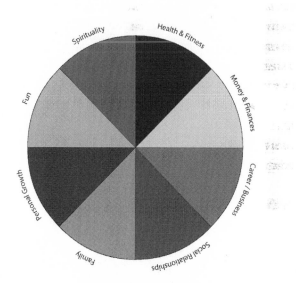

Figure: The Wheel of Life

Another popular way to think about our life is in broader terms of body, soul, and spirit. But I find these classes too vague to be actionable. Body breaks down to health and fitness; soul breaks down to mind and emotion; mind breaks down to learning and development while emotion breaks down to relationships and love and so on. After much breaking down and classification, you wind up with something similar to the Wheel of Life anyway.

The Wheel of Life provides a straightforward and clear lens through which we can reflect on our lives. And it provides enough detail to cover the bases but not too much to become overwhelming or lose its universal application.

The wheel is primarily used by coaches and personal development professionals as a scoring sheet for people; a means to measure how well you are doing in each segment of the wheel. For example, you could be doing great in career, but your family life might need improvement. Or you could be doing fantastic in health and fitness but really struggling spiritually.

As useful as this may be, for our purposes, we will not be focusing on scoring *you*, we will use it rather unconventionally as a scoring sheet for your *goals*. The goals that cover the most important segments will be the top contenders for your Big Goal. You will find these by using the Big Goal System Chart.

HOW TO GET TO THE BIG GOALS

The chart is easy to use. The first column lays out the segments of life. The next column asks you to weigh each segment from 1 to 3:

- 1 means the segment is mildly important to you at this time
- 2 means moderate importance
- 3 means the segment is vitally important to you at this point

	Weight (1-3)	Candidate #1 (1 - 3)	Candidate #2 (1 - 3)	Candidate #3 (1 - 3)	Candidate #4 (1 - 3)	Candidate #5 (1 - 3)
Health and Fitness						
Family						
Finances						
Work and Career						
Social Life						
Personal Development						
Hobbies and Recreation						
Spiritual Development						
Total						

Figure: The Big Goal System Chart

Take some time to reflect on your life and use the insights you gain to fill out this column first.

On the top row, there are five cells where you write your goal candidates. There are only five slots and they are called "candidates" because the aim is to get them down to three big goals in keeping with TVF. Being forced to choose a smaller number of goals to assess using the Big Goal System encourages us to think past the surface and choose the deeply important goals that show the most promise.

We will deal with the how of effectively articulating goals to increase your chances of success later in this chapter. But for now, a simple statement like "write a business plan for my side hustle" or "complete a professional certification" will suffice. At this point, they are candidates anyway so there is no need to obsess over wording too much. Go ahead and write your five candidates down in these slots.

Next, you will go down each candidate column and assign a score from 0 - 2 for each one corresponding to each segment of your wheel of life. Assign 0 for a goal that will have no direct impact on that category, 1 for moderate impact and 2 for high impact.

For example, let's say you set a goal to complete the requirements for a professional certification. This will score high in the category of career (probably 2) but low for health and fitness (probably 0). If you had weighted health and fitness as 3, and work and career as 2, you would then enter the numbers as follows:

- A score of 4 for Work and Career (score of 2 for the goal multiplied by a weight of 2 for the life segment)
- A score of 0 for health and fitness (score of 0 for the goal multiplied by a weight of 3 for health and fitness)

This makes sense because short of a huge leap in the imagination, the goal of securing a professional certification does not address your health and fitness. Unless it's a certification in health and fitness, but you know what I mean. For most, a score 0 for health and fitness is appropriate. Speaking of leaps in the imagination, avoid them—at least for this exercise.

Steps, not leaps

Let us continue with our hypothetical of the professional certification goal to illustrate the importance of not taking leaps while considering the impacts of our goal candidates on our life segments.

While it is plausible that the extra money you gain from the promotion that comes from completing a professional certification will pay for higher-quality fresh and healthy food as well as a premium gym membership, while also giving you more independence in your work to spare the time to actually use it, this is quite a leap. It is, in fact, three steps (or one huge leap) from your health and fitness segment.

Certification—Promotion—More money and time—Exercise and better nutrition.

These steps are also each potential goals all by themselves leading to a veritable confoundment of the entire exercise. On the other hand, the advancement in career is only one step from the goal, making it a more reasonable and defensible connection to make.

It is tempting to let the imagination run wild while making these connections but as much as possible, keep the associations to one step. If you find a goal candidate presents a compelling two-step association with a life segment, I recommend scoring the two-step associations lower than the one-step ones. Otherwise, your scores in each segment will be too close to be useful in helping you highlight what your big goals should be.

Overall, aim for *direct* associations. For this example, while the certification *could eventually* lead to a promotion and boost in income, it does not guarantee it. The only thing it really guarantees is increased competency. This is good for your career regardless. If I were scoring this, I would score 2 on work and career, and 1 on personal development. I would score the rest of the categories 0.

Even though a certification looks like it could impact the finances segment, until the certification goal is attained, finances are likely not flowing in. So, save that category for next time when you have a goal to get a promotion or switch careers on the strength of the (completed) certification.

With these guides in place, go ahead now and score each candidate under each life segment.

Adding it up to the big goals

When all the columns are filled out, simply add up your scores. The top three become your big goals. These are the goals that impact the most important aspects of your life presently as you have determined for yourself. They are, therefore, the best goals for you to pursue at this point in time. You might find that these big goals align perfectly with what you want to work and focus on. If so, terrific!

On the other hand, looking at what the chart says, you might feel the tug to work on some other more emotionally appealing goal. Perhaps the results are not what you feel you want. If you are confident in your weighting and scoring, then this might be just the insight you needed to help you redirect your efforts to what really matters to you.

GOAL-SETTING MODELS

If you have read any books, attended any workshops or seminars, or even just done a web search on the topic of goal setting, you certainly have encountered SMART goals. SMART forms the acronym for the criteria for setting a goal with the best chance of success. It breaks down as:

- Specific
- Measurable
- Attainable
- Result-oriented[4]
- Time-bound

For example, *I will read more books* does not pass as a SMART goal. It's not specific (what kind of books?). Neither is it measurable

---

[4] R is sometimes defined as "Relevant". However, since this is part of a discussion on defining a Big Goal, relevance is a given.

(how many books?). I suppose it is attainable but without being measurable, how would one know? As for being result-oriented, that's a tricky one we will explore later in this chapter. Lastly, it is clearly not time-bound (read more books by when?).

Here is a better goal statement: *I will read one book a month from each of the genres of business, parenting, spirituality, and science for the next 12 months.*

You see immediately that not only is this more specific and measurable, it also scores higher on every other criterion and is a much more defined and well-considered goal. On top of that, on closer examination, you might have also caught a whiff of the beginnings of an action plan. These are the features that make the SMART model so pervasive, enticing, and effective.

This example goal is actually one of mine from a few years ago. I had been wanting to read more books for a long time but never got as much traction as I wanted. Life was busy. But once I articulated the goal this way, I was able to make a lot more progress and tapped into some latent creativity to address the challenges that had me stymied in the past.

For example, to solve the challenge of time, I started reading books on long walks and train rides. I also started listening to audiobooks whenever I was doing chores. To solve the problem of access, I joined the local library and got access to an immense store of useful material. And the definition of genres helped regulate any analysis paralysis that such a vast collection would have otherwise created.

In short, using the SMART model proved very effective for me and I continue to apply it in other areas.

But while the SMART goal model is the most popular, there are other models. For example, there is the CLEAR model (Collaborative, Limited, Emotional, Appreciable and Refineable). And then there is the PURE model too (Positive, Understood, Relevant and Ethical).

To complicate matters further, the elements of these models seem to shift depending on what you are reading or listening to.

For example, while the "A" and "R" in SMART are usually defined as "Achievable" and "Result-oriented", I have also seen versions where they are defined as "Agreed" and "Realistic". I have even been part of a seminar where the speaker defined the "R" in SMART as wRitten (as he spelled it out) to make the point that your goals should not just live in your head but be penned down.[5] For the CLEAR model, I have seen minor deviations such as switching the "R" for a different meaning, and I have also seen complete overhauls. The most notable was an article I came across online where the *entire* acronym had been changed from the breakdown above to Challenging, Legal, Environmentally sound, Appropriate, and Recorded.

Clearly, these models are considered tools not only for goal setting but also for creativity with acronyms.

To be fair, acronyms are useful as mnemonic devices, especially when they are clever enough to spell the quality of the goal that they attempt to induce; who doesn't want their goals to be smart? And no one who knows even a little about goal setting would set out to create a goal that was deliberately *un*clear. As for pure, honestly, my first thought when I encountered this one was *gimme a break*. But after looking closely, it too panned out as bringing something to the table. It appears that for any single shortcoming of an existing acronym, a new one (or new version of the same one) pops up to fill the gap.

The result is more mnemonics than can be memorized.

Granted, a good acronym can help us remember the criteria for setting goals, but their real usefulness is the same as for most mental models. From the PASS model (Pull, Aim, Squeeze, Sweep)

---

[5] The speaker was actually me. Yes, I too have massaged acronyms to my will for the sake of making a point. But in my defence, there is plenty of evidence showing how important it is to write your personal goals down. It raises the odds that they will be achieved.

used to communicate how to use a fire extinguisher, to the ABC of sales success (Always Be Closing), it's not what they tell us about *what* to think, but about *how* to think that is most useful.

Whether you want your goals to be SMART or CLEAR or even PURE, the main point is *how* you think and how much thinking you do about the goal that really matters. And that boils down to two core qualities of good goals—they are *defined* and *deliberate*. Both of these are too long to create a coherent and memorable acronym. Believe me, I've tried.

In short, good goals have been thoroughly thought through, and then lucidly articulated. Bad goals are undefined, unrefined and often, unwRitten.

That said, acronyms and models for goal setting continue to offer immense value by providing a substrate for the crystallization of our otherwise ethereal goals. You don't want to leave the articulation of something so important as a Big Goal to chance, after all.

In choosing a model, my recommendation is the one that I have found has the most sophisticated motivational and operational machinery running under its hood, while still maintaining a plain-looking external. It is simultaneously the most simple and versatile. In a word, it is the most elegant of the models I have encountered. It's not perfect, of course, no single framework really is but it seems to work well, and it is the SMART choice.

SM: Specific and Measurable

I have lumped these two criteria of the SMART model together because it's tough to do one well without inadvertently checking the box on the other one, if only partly. These two conditions help define the goal. If you were an archer, these are the bullseye you're aiming for.

To illustrate, goals like "earn more money" or "lose weight" are too general to be useful. They are neither specific nor measurable.

The question becomes how much money? Or how much weight? But both can be improved with a few tweaks. Earn more money can be improved to "increase my income by X amount" or "increase the earnings from my side hustle by 50%". And instead of just aiming to "lose weight", set a target weight—a measurable *number* in pounds or kilograms.

Defining a specific and measurable target overthrows that surreptitious vagueness that plagues many goals and installs focus in its stead. It helps us overcome a subtle self-sabotaging pitfall—the avoidance of clarity as a means of dodging commitment and accountability; in short, the fear of failure.

There is no wiggling out of whether or not you achieved a specific and measurable goal. You either did or you didn't. You either earned the amount or you didn't; lost the weight, or you didn't. Numbers don't have feelings and they certainly do not listen to excuses. And that creates fear. What if I fail? What if I don't have what it takes? So you set vague goals so you don't feel the pressure that comes with the clarity.

The answer to this is to remember that you own the goal and not the other way around. A goal should never tyrannize. It should instead motivate you by giving a clear target—something to shoot for, something to aim at, an end to achieve. The clarity should serve as a benefit, not a drawback. In TVF terms, it helps you define what you should be focusing on in order to achieve the goal. And on the subject of achievement, let's look next at the A in SMART.

A: Achievable/Attainable

This aspect of the SMART acronym speaks directly to motivation. Few things will tire a person out and sap their motivation faster than the pursuit of an objective that they perceive to be impossible.

When it comes to goals, you're better off building capacity by setting easy goals to begin with, hitting them, and then increasing the difficulty incrementally. This is especially true when entering uncharted territory. Again, pressure sets in—not the good kind that motivates you to push, but the bad kind that leaves you feeling anxious and defeated before you even start.

So, when deciding on a goal, make sure you have enough faith in yourself to achieve it. There is a reason high-jumpers don't set the bar at the highest point on their first jump. I think late Hall of Fame soul musician Bill Withers puts it nicely when he said, "You can't get to 'wonderful' without passing through 'all right'".

R: Result-oriented

The predominant thinking around this stipulation for SMART goals is that your goal needs to be oriented or articulated in a way that makes its evaluation based on a defined *outcome*, not a *process*. For example, the goal to cut your weight by 20lbs is result-oriented. The goal to work out three times a week is not. The desired result is the leaner body so that is what the goal should be oriented towards, *not* the process or the actions you take. I partly agree—but only partly.

I agree because staying result-oriented helps us pivot and remain flexible in our approach where needed. With the result being the target, we can stay motivated on that outcome and not get mired in processes. We are also more open to changing processes altogether if needed. Plus, a bunch of work with no results to show for it is a hard sell.

But on the flip side, there is a great deal of motivational torque you can generate by treating a well-designed process as a goal of its own.

For example, in writing this book, the desired result is obviously a published book. But that won't happen without a process of writing. The process will involve producing a certain volume of writing regularly. There aren't many options short of hiring a ghostwriter—to publish a book, write you must! As for not having anything to show, well, consider this: even if after weeks and weeks of writing, a book never panned out, if done well, the process would have improved me in other ways—increased my writing skills or discipline perhaps.[6] In this sense, there is a lot of value in setting a process goal for writing a book. The goal may take the form of writing a certain number of words daily or weekly.

If that word-count goal sounds like a result-oriented goal in itself with the result being the number of words produced, you just nailed the issue with setting process goals—the proliferation of goals; goals nested in goals each with its own mini-result feeding into a larger goal…ad infinitum. At this point in goal setting, we go cross-eyed and want to jump out a window. But our own good judgement will restore reason and talk us off the ledge.

Just remember that your goals should not tyrannize but clarify and motivate. With this in mind, you can take the following approach which I use often with good results.

Set your big goal in the old-fashioned, result-oriented way. Then set process goals that lead to it. Next, choose checkpoints for when you will revisit your progress to see how things are going. Depending on the timeframe for the big goal, your check-ins can be daily, weekly or monthly. A goal with a six-month timeframe could have weekly check-ins for example.

Businesses call this pre-set check-in period the "time horizon"—the period they will allow a certain approach to a business goal to work unhampered before they re-evaluate it and decide whether to keep, tweak, or trash it. You can do the same.

If during your check-in you find that the process you implemented to move you toward your goal is working, renew it,

---

[6] This is an anchor point in books like Scott Adam's *How to Fail at Almost Everything and Still Win Big* and similar books' critique of traditional, result-centric goal-setting: the idea that who you become on the way to achieving your goal is just as important (perhaps more so) as the attainment of the goal. So, it makes more sense to make the process the goal rather than the outcome. Focus on *becoming* rather than achieving.

set the next check-in, and push forward. If it's not working, see what your options are and adjust accordingly.

This approach to results is like having milestones on the journey to a destination. They help us keep on track and motivated without sacrificing our freedom to take a different route if needed. Your mileage may vary, but this approach will serve you well regardless.

T: Time-bound

Let me ask you a question: How productive are you three months before a deadline? How about three days before?

If you tend to be more productive the closer you get to a deadline, then you have just hit on the genius behind making your goal time-bound. Napoleon Hill, the writer of one of the most influential and top-selling personal development books of the last two centuries, *Think and Grow Rich*, is quoted as saying, "A goal is a dream with a deadline." Without setting a time parameter for what you want to achieve, you run the risk of never achieving it.

Time-boundedness makes goals real and realizable. Making a goal time-bound also helps with motivation. While being overly aggressive with the time frame can be a recipe for discouragement if the goal is not achieved, a healthy deadline can work wonders for focus, motivation, and creativity. Knowing that there is a set date in the future when you will step on the scale, review your bank statement, or take a blood cholesterol test will motivate you to do what it takes now—exercise, create income streams, or eat more mindfully as the case may be. It will also help you plan since you have a set time in the future to work backwards from and align your forward actions against.

One of the reasons the goal statement I used when I wanted to read more was so effective was because it had two time elements built in—a monthly one and one for the end of the year. You can use this principle too if your goal accommodates it. In any case, when you set your big goals, make sure to set a time for completion as well. It's ok if you need to adjust here and there—just avoid the temptation to leave the goal without a set time for completion.

Overall, the key point to keep in mind is that a good goal statement answers the question of *what, by when?* In using the SMART model, SMAR answers the "what"; T answers the "by when". You need both elements to give yourself the best chance of achieving your goals. This becomes even more important when the stakes are high, as they will be with your Big Goals.

BOOK II
TVF DISCIPLINES

*"It is better to be patient than powerful. It is better to
win control over yourself than over whole cities."*

Proverbs 16:32

The quality of our lives is a reflection of how we live day-to-day. Living the TVF way means that we not only reorganize our lives around our Vital Few, but also that we develop a Vital Few set of disciplines.

This part of the book first explores the discipline mindset itself as a key part of TVF. We then discuss the Vital Few disciplines—the practices that produce the most results. Finally, we look into ways to incorporate TVF disciplines into our lives so that we can reap all the benefits they promise.

CHAPTER 8

Can Making Your Bed Change Your Life?

In 2014, Admiral Bill McRaven, a decorated Navy Seal officer, gave an inspirational commencement address at the University of Texas at Austin which went viral. The title on the University of Texas YouTube channel for the speech is simply, *University of Texas at Austin 2014 Commencement Address*—so far, so boring. But not long after the address, many videos popped up online with a different title theme around some version of "If You Want To Change The World, Start By Making Your Bed".

At the time of this publication, the speech in its most popular iterations has over 30 million views, and that's on YouTube alone. It's fair to say that the video has been viewed by a lot of people across various platforms. This is an impressive feat, especially considering the genre—commencement speeches not delivered by pop superstars don't usually spread far and wide online. That's usually the domain of quirky, risqué, and colourful music videos. That this speech spread like wildfire showed that it delivered a message which was meaningful and helpful to many people. So, what exactly was that message?

The speech begins with a few humorous anecdotes and then dives into ten lessons from military training to help the graduates change the world. It was the first lesson, however, that formed the basis of most of the videos that spun off from the original—the call to make your bed. The message was simple enough; achievement, the kind that can change the world, begins with discipline. And it begins with the little acts of discipline we perform every single day.

The first victory is the victory over the little elements of chaos in our lives, like a messy bed. Discipline is at the center of this idea; exercising discipline over ourselves is the key to the self-mastery that can empower us to change the world around us.

Coming from an Admiral, the message is poignant, powerful, and credible. As Admiral McRaven himself describes, the training that goes into becoming a soldier is gruelling. If there's one profession that personifies the concept of discipline, it's the military. No one can sell the idea of discipline as effectively as our men and women in uniform. So synonymous is the military with discipline that whenever we want to depict the quality, we opt for a picture of a soldier. A close second is an athlete—a marathon runner perhaps.

But rarely do we use an image of a software programmer, nurse, writer, artist, or parent. Yet these other professions demand discipline as well. Perhaps not the same spartan brand as is demanded of a Navy Seal or an endurance athlete, but discipline all the same. This was the thrust of that epic commencement address delivered in 2014—discipline is critical to success, regardless of your calling.

Discipline is what gives form and order to so many other resources in life.

Time without discipline leads to unproductivity. Money, power, and even good intentions without discipline can quickly lead to ruin. And talent without discipline is a recipe for short-lived unsustainable spurts of success. But talent, even a little ability, coupled with discipline can create amazing results. More importantly, it can *sustain* it.

This is because while discipline may start out as something you merely do, it soon evolves into something you become.

DISCIPLINE DEFINED

Discipline is one of those words that means different things in different contexts. But to get to the root of the meaning, let's get to the root of the word itself. It comes from the Latin word *disciplina* which means "instruction" or "training". That's why branches of study such as medicine, sociology, engineering and law are referred to as disciplines. They train the disciple in a method of seeing and behaving which is in line with the tenets of that field.

In its evolution through the ages, however, the word discipline has taken on a macabre meaning. Specifically, in the middle ages, it became associated with the act of self-mortification. This latter meaning is probably responsible for the word taking on a rather repulsive air. After all, self-mortification is not a pleasant prospect by a long way. Yet, it is not hard to see how training and instruction—especially at the level of rigour and vigour required for mastery—can begin to resemble a form of punishment.

However, to focus our minds on the benefits and value of discipline, we need to divorce it from its darker associations and reunite it to its older, more aspirational meaning. Which is the pursuit of mastery through a willing commitment to a system of instruction and training. The ultimate end of this instruction or training is to bring form and order to a situation with the aim of achieving a goal. The instruction of a running coach brings order and form to running. Through well-thought-out and structured exercise regimens, the otherwise unruly and flailing limbs of the athlete are disciplined to work in concert to achieve speeds that most of us could only dream of.

For you, discipline might not mean hours on the track, though it very well might. But it *will* involve bringing order and form to a situation in your life in a way that produces an outcome that you desire and deem beneficial.

Three conditions are needed for the exercise of discipline:

1. A current state of affairs that defines how we are doing. How much we weigh, how much we earn, how much we own, how much energy or enthusiasm we feel, how punctual we are for meetings, how connected we feel to our loved ones, how high we can kick, or how fast we can run or swim. The current state tells us where we are starting from.

2. A desired state (standards, expectations, or goals). The desired state is the end goal; how much we *want* to weigh, earn, or own in comparison to the current state of affairs. It is, by definition, different from the current state of affairs. Without this difference, there would be no need for action or discipline.

3. Mediating and moderating adjustments (MAMAs). These are the changes we make to our actions, emotions, and mindsets that help us close the gap between the current state of affairs and the desired state. MAMAs mediate between our current and desired state by moderating our behaviour; when we need to exercise restraint versus when to exert ourselves; when to remain equanimous versus when to respond with emphatic action. In other words, they orient us to our goals. Without MAMAs, we couldn't navigate from our current state of affairs to our desired state.

As goal-oriented beings, virtually every action we take is intended to close the gap between some current and desired state. The current state of being in bed versus being at the office, for example, will encompass many orienting actions—get out of bed, brush your teeth, dress, walk, commute, etc. Each one of these can be further broken down into current and desired states of their own; the current state of pyjamas versus business attire, for example. But all these mini-goals are subsumed not only by the goal of getting to work, but also perhaps a bigger goal of career or business advancement. Discipline is what gets you out of bed when you'd rather sleep not because of a goal of physically relocating yourself to an office, but because of the larger goal of achieving progress in your work and attaining the benefits that come with it.

Discipline is the willful alignment of our thoughts and actions to the mediating and moderating behaviours that close the gap between our current and desired state. It is choosing actions, thoughts, and mindsets that bring us closer to where we want to be. Discipline is doing what MAMA says. It's what makes the disciple show up in the first place, and stay, and study, and follow instruction and practice, perhaps painful in the moment, in pursuit of a future benefit.

This brings us to a deeper definition of discipline—one that goes beyond the instruction the disciple receives from the outside to the quality she possesses on the inside. That is, the quality of self-control. It is this ability to delay gratification and master the self that is the backbone of discipline. And, as we shall see in the next sections, it is a vital quality for success.

LESSONS FROM DUNEDIN

One of the most ambitious studies on human behaviour in history was initiated in Dunedin, New Zealand in the 1970s. When I say this study was ambitious, I'm not joking. As of 2020, about half a century later, the experiment is still going on, has produced over 1300 publications and has given rise to sub-studies in family health, parenting, and generational dynamics. Perhaps, appropriately as ambitious is what the study sought to determine—what quality is the single most important indicator of success?

To answer this question, the study traced the lives of over 1,000 individuals from early childhood. The participants in the study were spread across social, economic, and gender spectra. The one area they did not vary in though, was age—all participants were born within 12 months of each other, placing them all at approximately the same age.

What did they find? The differentiator and the factor that most consistently predicts a child's success in later life is the child's degree of self-control. What the study called the "ability to delay gratification". In one word, discipline.

At one of the checkpoints during the Dunedin study, when the participants were about 32 years old, the researchers compared how they had fared in life in the areas of their physical wellbeing, finances, and criminal behaviour—what the researchers termed "health, wealth, and public safety". What they found was instructive; to quote the report:

> ...childhood self-control predicts physical health, substance dependence, personal finances, and criminal offending outcomes, following a gradient of self-control. Effects of children's self-control could be disentangled from their intelligence and social class.

While this result might be surprising at first, a little consideration will reveal that it makes perfect sense. A lot of people with terrific starts in life manage to make a mess of it all. Conversely, there are books filled with inspirational stories of people who despite having a rough start, still manage to build enviable lives. Smart people with high IQs can still wind up not amounting to much while people with average or even modest IQs can rise high in life.

The factor that determines how well you do with the hand you have been dealt is discipline. It's what helps you regulate all your other abilities and marshal your powers in the service of your goals. When at a disadvantage, discipline can help you surmount difficulty and when advantages are in place, discipline provides an added edge.

As the report stated under the section on the impact of self-control on finances (emphasis mine):

> Although the study members' social class of origin and IQ were strong predictors of their adult socioeconomic status and income, poor self-control offered *significant incremental validity* in predicting the socioeconomic position they achieved and the income they earned.

If you want to greatly increase your chances of not only living effectively by the TVF way but also living effectively *period*, developing discipline is vital. This makes the development of discipline a compelling pursuit. Thankfully, the amount of discipline you possess, unlike your parent's bank account balance at your birth, is something you can influence and improve. Discipline *can* be developed. And since we have begun our exploration in New Zealand, let's skip over to Sydney, Australia to see what another set of influential researchers can tell us about this discipline dynamic.

THE EXPANSION OF DISCIPLINE

In an insightful experiment by Meg Oaten and Ken Cheng, it was shown that when people participate in activities that exercise their self-control, or what I call discipline, they were more likely to display self-control in other areas of their lives.

Participants were recruited by the researchers and asked to keep a detailed track of their spending. As the researchers noted, money is an area in which people have been shown experimentally to lack self-control. The expansion of access to credit cards and the proliferation of the "buy now, pay later" approach to finances in North America and much of the West has caused a lot of individuals and households considerable stress.

In addition, the bombardment of non-stop ads—from the ones that litter our beloved YouTube cat videos to the ones that fill every available billboard space in our cities—has made us acutely aware not of all the many blessings and privileges we enjoy but instead of the shiny new things we manifestly do not. Hence, as the researchers surmised, getting people to exercise self-control over their finances in modern-day North America would be a true stretch of their self-control.

The participants in the study were required to submit their financial statements for review by the experimenters. The researchers then developed a personalized financial plan for each of them, complete with a detailed diary which the participant was required to fill in dutifully. This diary also included questions intended to test how much strain the activity of tracking spending imposed.

Judging by entries in the diaries such as, "I really want to buy a car, but it is so hard banking each week because I feel like I am missing out on so many things..." or "...I pretty much have to stay indoors... I have to use my willpower..." I think it's safe to say there was plenty of stretching going on.

But there was one other thing they were required to do which the researchers hoped would shine a light on the effects they were interested in. Every month for four months while the financial monitoring was going on, the participants were to report to the lab and complete a difficult visual tracking task (VTT)—one that was designed to test their powers of self-control. The task involved tracking fast-moving black squares on a white screen. As if that wasn't hard enough, there was another screen in plain sight playing a hilarious comedy routine.

Imagine for a second you were one of these participants—would you have a hard time? Indulge, even for a second, in the entertainment, and you'd lose track of the squares and fail the task. Focus on the boring, monochromatic squares, miss out on the fun. Odds are you would fail many times and have to employ a lot of discipline to successfully accomplish the task. And even then, you would still find it incredibly difficult. Well, so did the participants. At least initially.

Over the four months of exercising self-control in their finances (evidenced by the detailed logs and bank statements reviewed by the experimenters), they showed significant improvement in their abilities to focus and complete the tracking task. A control group who came in just as frequently and performed the tracking test on the same schedule (but without the financial tracking exercise) showed no improvement.

It became clear that the exercise of self-control in their finances had improved their ability to exercise self-control in completing the difficult visual tracking task. The impact of the financial tracking exercise on improved self-control was rendered more compelling as participants began showing improvements in the VTT in as little as one month. As the researcher's state in their paper:

> ...adherence to the financial monitoring program made people less vulnerable to the general tendency for self-control to deteriorate quickly in response to immediate demands.

In other words, exercising discipline in one aspect of life makes you more able to do so in other areas. That alone is fantastic news. But it gets better.

As the same researchers demonstrated in a different experiment involving exercising self-control in sticking to a fitness regimen, as you persist in your goals, you are likely to report other unexpected, positive changes. You might find yourself procrastinating less in general, keeping your house cleaner, eating healthier, and even getting better at controlling your temper.

The great insight here is that improving discipline by exercising self-control in one aspect of your life makes you more likely to apply the discipline to other aspects, *even in areas you did not anticipate*, and—drawing from our lessons from Dunedin—help you live a better life overall.

HOW TO INCREASE DISCIPLINE

Like a muscle, discipline can be strengthened and enlarged. But also like a muscle, discipline can be overworked, over-trained, and exhausted. Perhaps worst of all, discipline can be ignored and left to atrophy to the ultimate detriment of the individual. The growing body of research we have explored along with countless anecdotal accounts including that of Admiral McRaven point to these conclusions. But they also point to a simple and effective method for developing discipline—exercising self-control in the things we can control, starting with small things and then building up our capacity.

If you want to develop discipline, start exercising self-control like you would exercise a muscle. Start slowly but consistently, then build up gradually. You don't start bench-pressing 300lbs on your first day in the gym or running at full blast on the treadmill for a straight hour. That's just a recipe for injury and a guarantee you will be out of the gym licking your wounds for a long time after. Instead, you pick a simple exercise and manage the load of weights, resistance, or intensity so that you feel sufficient strain to challenge yourself while still leaving enough energy to return to train again the next day.

Pick a habit that you know will demand sufficient strain. Researchers have shown that even so-called "little" habits like fixing your posture can provide a good enough work out for your discipline to help you grow in self-control. Below I recommend a straightforward progression of exercises for implementing this advice.

Self-contained discipline exercises

These are little changes you make to one (and only one) aspect of your behaviour, hence the name self-contained. You expend your energy on only *one* thing. For example, you might decide to alter an aspect of your speech pattern—saying "yes" instead of "yeah" or speaking only in complete sentences. As a public-speaking coach, one that comes up a lot with clients is speaking without any unintentional filler words (um, ah, so, like, etc.). This is effective for training your discipline muscle with fairly low stakes and effort expenditure but with a potentially high-return—enough for some strain on the muscle, but not too much to cause breakdown or utter fatigue. The upshot is that the more you exercise, the stronger you become and the higher your threshold for fatigue becomes.

Below is a list of effective and immediately actionable self-contained discipline exercises:

- ❏ Fixing your posture when walking or sitting at your desk
- ❏ Speaking without filler words
- ❏ Speaking in complete sentences
- ❏ Slowing down when you handwrite
- ❏ Commuting without headphones or cell-phone usage
- ❏ Wiping down your shoes before and after each wear
- ❏ Altering the sound of your laugh
- ❏ Threading your belt through your pants in the opposite direction
- ❏ Laying out your clothes the night before you intend to wear them
- ❏ Brushing your teeth with your non-dominant hand (any routine action using your non-dominant hand should do, just keep it to a short time)

The list could go on but I'm sure you have already seen that any one of the little day-to-day actions you perform in a certain way are good candidates for a self-contained discipline exercise. What is essential is that the exercise forces you to go against your own grain in some way—to alter how you perform something you are used to doing in a certain way already. The two I started with (and still use) are the deliberate handwriting and any related to speech pattern disruption. You might find others more appealing to you and, of course, you can always make some up for yourself.

Just be sure it's simple, self-contained, and something you do regularly enough to ensure you get to exercise daily.

Multi-step exercises

Routines are strings of actions that create patterns. Your morning routine, for example, may include waking up, turning off your alarm, getting out of bed, walking to the bathroom, throwing water on your face, brushing your teeth, etc. These patterns can be so ingrained that they run automatically without our conscious awareness and we can find ourselves frustrated at attempts to disrupt them. What I call multi-step discipline exercises involve either significant changes to established patterns (as opposed to just single, self-contained actions), or the development of new routines altogether.

Both disruptions to existing patterns and the development of new ones build discipline and both are significantly more demanding than a self-contained discipline exercise.

For example, you might decide to disrupt your morning routine by inserting the action of downing a glass of water after turning your alarm off and then inserting ten minutes of stretching and body-weight resistance training after getting out of bed. Alternatively, you might develop a whole new routine of exercise or sleep such as going to the gym three times a week or instituting a new regular sleep and wake schedule. Oh, and you should definitely start making your bed, of course.

As a discipline training device, the principles of starting small and starting slow remain, regardless of whether you are using self-contained or multi-step exercises. It's easier to slightly alter an action you are already used to performing than it is to alter an existing pattern. And altering an existing pattern is easier than creating a whole new pattern of different actions.

As you start to exercise your discipline in these different ways, over time, you will develop immense capacity in self-regulation and discipline. You will also have a neat track record of victories that will boost your confidence. Most importantly, you will build up power and stamina in your discipline so that you can better exert or restrain yourself when it matters most.

SELF-GRATIFICATION AND THE VITAL FEW

In pursuing the lifestyle of living by your Vital Few, you will be faced with times when distraction is easier than focus; when procrastination is more appealing than working on your goals; when immediate gratification feels more satisfying (albeit temporarily) than holding out for the long run and big gains. Don't give in.

This gets even harder when working on our Vital Few demands radical changes to what we spend most of our time doing. Our old habits will tug at us, sometimes rather violently. We can feel torn or even dissonant at times, but those are just growing pains.

As we build the ability to delay gratification and stand by our Vital Few, we will soon start building this muscle and it will get easier. We may falter now and again, but that's Ok. As long as we learn from the experience and recompose ourselves, we will continue to make progress.

Can Vs. should

The Vital Few way of life is entrenched in discipline—in what we choose *not* to do as much as what we do. But more and more, choosing what *not* to do is hard. It used to be that we were very limited in what we could pursue; access to information and resources was limited largely by our geographic location. But thanks to the internet and the connections it enables, these days, we can take up any interest, immerse ourselves in any online community vigorously discussing everything from TV shows to tailored clothing. Reddit, the largest collection of forums online, is the 6th most popular site in the US and 18th in the world. Topics on Reddit vary from the broad to the incredibly niche to the downright bizarre with an entire subreddit dedicated to birds with arms.

Does your new interest need some knowledge? Take an online course. SkillShare, one of the most popular online course sites boasts over 28,000 courses from pet portrait drawing to programming in python. Udemy boasts over 100,000 courses! Both are relatively inexpensive and accessible from anywhere with an internet connection. And while you are going through the course, if you find you need some gear to make your programming or doggy-drawing dreams a reality, you can visit a vast array of online stores. A few (or few hundred) dollars later and you have the basic knowledge and gear to start down a new path. On a budget? Replace the online course with videos on YouTube and opt for Craig's List or Kijiji and you can be on your way for cheap.

Whatever your fancy, you can pursue it. And while this has opened up many powerful and positive possibilities, it has also introduced some perils for the person seeking to maximize effectiveness through the adoption of the timeless principle of less is more. Now, perhaps more than ever, discipline is critical.

Discipline helps us separate *can* from *should*. Just because you can, doesn't mean you should. And even if you should, the question becomes is this the right time? Is this a part of your Vital Few *now*? Or it is better suited for later? In this sense, discipline simplifies our lives and helps preserve our sanity. And it does this, in part, by helping us decide.

CHAPTER 9

The World of Decisions

Imagine yourself on a scenic, serene nature trail. Lush greenery lines the footpath ahead and you can hear the faint sound of lapping waves and children's laughter in the distance. A cool breeze whistles through from ahead, its tender tentacles brushing over you as it passes by. It carries the clean scent of saltwater. You stop for a second and drink it in, gently closing your eyes. Then you continue on until you arrive at a narrow three-pronged fork in the road. What path do you choose? The left, right or middle?

This might seem like an inconsequential decision. Most likely, you'll be fine regardless of your choice. But those three paths, though seemingly separated by only a few feet of distance, might be worlds apart.

There is a thought in theoretical physics that is fast gaining ground in mainstream. It challenges the long-held notion of a singular universe and suggests that there are instead a countless number of universes, dubbed the multiverse. Proponents of this "multiverse theory" say there are an infinite number of parallel worlds to ours and that many are popping in and out of existence all the time. These parallel universes, they submit, exist in an infinitely larger space referred to rather curiously as "the bulk".

As if that wasn't mind-bending enough, there are different versions of you, me and everyone else in these different universes with each version of us supposedly created as a result of (along with some other potential factors) each new decision we make. In our little imaginary stroll to the beach from earlier, not one but actually three of "you" arrive based on the choice of paths. On top of that, the "three yous" arrive at three separate beaches in three separate parallel worlds—perhaps each with its own set of freshly minted sand-castling juveniles. Think of *that* the next time you pick your route to drive home from work.

There is much more to be discovered before we can say whether this theory is right or wrong. As one may imagine, it is prohibitively difficult to prove conclusively in a lab. And instinctively, it's hard to conceive of an *infinite* number of worlds somewhere *out there*.

But there is one aspect of the theory that I find I can accept with virtually zero struggle—the idea that our decisions create new realities. To explain, let us take another excursion into the field of etymology. I promise this one will be brief.

CUT OFF

The word "decision" is related to the word "incision". But while an incision is a cut into something, a decision is a cut *away* from something. Whenever you make a de-cision, you are *separating* from the myriad other ways you could act in that situation. So, a surgeon may make an incision into a particular area of the body during a medical procedure. But that choice is a decision that means she is not cutting into other areas of the patient, thankfully.

Making a decision means you choose one thing, one approach, one path, to the exclusion of all other options.

I told you it would be brief.

DISCIPLINE AND DECIDING IN ADVANCE

Decisiveness is the ability to choose a direction or course of action, often boldly and quickly. It is an exalted trait and a label of honour, especially for people in positions of leadership. Yet, there is nothing in the essential make-up of decisiveness that requires haste or urgency. On the contrary, as we shall see here, our best decisions are made in advance—they are thought through long before the situation where they are deployed.

We know that we are susceptible to an army of biases and weaknesses from inside and manipulations from the outside that can cause us to act against our best interests in the pressure of the moment. Knowing ourselves, we know better than to trust ourselves blindly.

This is why one of the most important disciplines you can develop is the habit of making as many of your decisions as possible in advance. This discipline affects all other habits. In fact, habit formation itself relies heavily on the discipline of deciding in advance.

DECIDING IN ADVANCE: THE VITAL HABIT

Habits have been with us for as long as we have been alive. However, recently, our attention has been refocused on this critical aspect of our lives thanks to the work of a few influential writers. Charles Duhigg's book, *The Power of Habit*, was a resounding literary and commercial success. At its heart was an old idea—the fact that our habits, those automatic acts and thoughts we perform unconsciously, are key to success in life. Bad habits, bad outcomes; good habits, good outcomes. Want to change your life? Get to work changing your habits.

Thankfully, his book goes beyond this and provides a valuable blueprint for *how* to change our habits. Since Duhigg's book, James Clear has written a useful book as well, *Atomic Habits*, where he drills down further into more granular habit-reforming tactics. Both books are well-written and thoroughly treat the subject of habits.

As important as habits are to success, and as much as I struggled whether or not to dedicate an entire chapter to the subject, I realize that others, not the least of which are Duhigg and Clear, have done a fantastic job of this already. Therefore, this section is not meant to provide an exhaustive exposition on the subject—for that, the two books above are excellent resources.

I agree completely that habits are pivotal to producing consistently positive outcomes, but even they lean on the vital concept of this chapter—deciding in advance.

How habits form

The habit circuitry is defined by the Cue-Routine-Reward loop. The cue might be the smell of freshly baked goods, the routine is you purchasing a donut, and the reward is the insidious sugar rush. Cue-routine-reward.

A more deliberately crafted and beneficial loop might be setting a reminder on your phone to cue you in the middle of the day to re-center yourself; the routine is a quiet minute of meditation and the reward is a sense of calm and wellbeing. Cue-routine-reward. That's easy enough.

But most people are interested not only in understanding how habits work but how to change bad ones and how to develop new (and better) ones. Well, when it comes to *changing* or *developing* new habits, one concept surfaces consistently—what I call deciding in advance.

How habits change

The strategy outlined by most experts to break a bad habit is to attack one or both of the cue or routine steps in the loop. Suffice to say that if you left your intervention till the end of the loop (the reward), it would be too late. So, the best approach is to work on the cue or the routine.

Eliminating the cue so the routine is never triggered is one way—don't walk by any confectioneries. Or keep the cue, but alter the routine—whenever you smell sweet baked goods, do ten jumping jacks and have a glass of water. Good luck with that by the way. In either case, though, you are either working on the cue or working on the routine.

However, in either approach, one of the surest ways to predict whether or not a person will be successful in developing or changing a habit is how much they rehearse their response to the cues for a bad habit, and how much forethought they give to the execution of the new one. The person who plans ahead in detail for both is a lot more likely to succeed.

How much more? Well, results from one study involving people trying to build an exercise habit indicated that having an implementation intention—essentially a statement articulating their advance decisions on how they will execute their plans—*doubled* their odds of following through on their exercise goals. Clearly, what matters more than whether you attack a cue or a routine is how much you decide in advance the details of the execution of the attack. That is, given a broad understanding of the habit loop, the vital ingredient that actually makes the difference in making useful and positive changes to our habits is the practice of deciding in advance.

Want to exercise more? Don't just plan to exercise three times a week. Decide in advance on what days, at what time and at what location you will exercise. Go even further by deciding in advance what gym clothes and shoes you will wear and even pick them out ahead of time. You could even drill down further to deciding the workouts in advance. To really kick this into high gear, decide in advance *how you will handle potential roadblocks.*

Example: I will pack three sets of gym clothes every weekend and leave my gym shoes at work and I will work out at lunch hour every Monday, Wednesday, and Friday at the gym two blocks from the office. *If an important meeting comes up that I cannot reschedule, I will go an hour earlier.*

Or maybe you want to practice more mindfulness, as I will encourage you to do in Chapter 10. Then don't just plan to meditate for 20 minutes a day. Decide when, where, and how in advance, and engineer your cues. Like in the example earlier, you can set an alarm, or tack the habit onto the end of an existing one like brushing your teeth. And, of course, decide how you will handle potential disruptions to your plans as well.

Making all these decisions in advance is the backbone for building new and better habits. But deciding in advance is not only at the core of changing our habits, it can also help us in that most universal and transferable of all business and personal skills—negotiation.

Deciding in advance: Negotiations

A few years ago, my wife and I went to buy a car. It was a used car but it looked to be in terrific shape. We didn't want it financed and so were paying cash. Just one problem—we had not made up our minds exactly *how* much we were willing to pay. Perhaps more importantly, we had not decided in advance how much we were *not* willing to pay. We knew vaguely that we would not pay asking price, but that was about it.

After meeting the seller, it became obvious that he had given this a lot of thought, much more than we had. As the negotiation unfolded, we found ourselves giving up more and more ground as we inched closer and closer to doing the unthinkable—paying the full asking price. The different human frailties and biases were in full swing and holding sway, though we might not have realized it at the time.

Fortunately for us, we *had* decided in advance that we would have our mechanic evaluate the car. Thankfully, he was on the other side of town. During the drive there, we had a chance to cool off and regroup, and we made some decisions on exactly what our walk-away point was. To help us even more, the mechanic found a minor issue with the brakes that would have required some money to correct. That gave us the much-needed leverage to drive the price down to a more comfortable number.

The seller didn't do badly either and both parties walked away happy. In fact, we all had a long friendly chat after the deal was sealed where we learned an important piece of information—what the seller did for a living. Turns out, he was a sales manager. This guy pretty much made a living on his mastery of negotiations. Without the fortunate sequence of events—the test drive and the brakes—we wouldn't have stood a chance against this professional. I guess you could say we had a lucky brake.

Negotiators know that to be successful, they have to decide in advance how much ground they are willing to give up. They speak about win-wins as the most desirable outcomes. They also speak of BATNAs (Best Alternative to a Negotiated Agreement), and resistance points—technical terms for "the point at which we walk away". Without deciding all these factors in advance, they would be leaving a lot up to either chance (something they can't really count), the goodwill of the other party (something they can't really count on), or their own rationality (something they definitely cannot count on).

When pressure mounts or when something unexpected happens, we can't trust ourselves 100% to make clear, rational decisions. So, the more we can decide in advance, the better our chances.

In an interaction where there is a trade of any kind, the person who has done more deciding in advance has a big advantage over the one who just shows up and wings it. Professional negotiators are trained to develop a clear picture of what outcome they want. They also consider all the possible directions the negotiation could go, including tactics the other side might employ so they can pivot and adapt seamlessly on the fly.

This might sound adversarial, but it doesn't have to be. A win-win situation is actually easier to achieve when both parties know a win is possible for them and they work towards it. A win-lose is almost the guaranteed default when one of the parties has not decided in advance.

And while all this might sound complicated, let me assure you that you probably employ these exact tactics already. Perhaps with your friends or family. Imagine yourself negotiating with your clever but rather lazy teen about cleaning her room:

Hmmm… if I ask her to clean her room, she might come back with a distraction about wanting to do her homework first. If she does that, I will concede that ground, but then get to her commit to a specific time when she will clean her room later today with no excuses. And I will hold her to it.

See? You are already good at deciding in advance. Now all you have to do is do it more intentionally, for more situations, and on purpose. You will increase the odds of your success in any negotiation, from what movies to watch to how much you get paid.

Deciding in advance and visualization

Visualization, a practice that science has shown over and over again to be key for peak performance, is an act of deciding in advance. It's the mental dimension of rehearsal that is just as important as any physical aspect of the rehearsal. Perhaps more so.

The athlete visualizes the play, the stroke, the kick, or the catch over and over. They visualize for success and against failure. They decide in advance how they will position and re-position to achieve their goal. And then they go one step further and train their bodies and minds to respond rapidly and accurately.

You can use this for *any* event or interaction you deem important enough to invest the effort in—a speech, a job interview, a wedding ceremony, anything. Play out all the plausible scenarios you can conceive in your imagination and brew your best responses for each. If any of the situations you foresaw do occur, you will be ready.

DECIDING IN ADVANCE CAN BE HARD

I will be the first to admit that deciding in advance is hard work. It involves a lot more forethought than comes naturally to most people. Most people are either 10,000ft people or 10ft people in their perspective. That is, they either speak and act in broad strokes and lose the resolution they need to execute effectively, or they have their noses so up close to the map that they cannot see the bigger picture.

Getting good at deciding in advance requires a flexible mindset—one that allows you to keep a bigger outcome in mind while anticipating detailed scenarios. I sometimes find myself stuck in one or the other of these extremes at different times and I have to consciously work to reset my perspective. Given how much work that has proven to be for me and how much benefit it produces, I find it interesting when people brag about their lack of detail-orientation. These individuals enjoy throwing out modish words like "strategist" or "visionary" which generally translate to "I'll come up with the idea and let someone else (I'll decide who later) take care of the details and execution of the idea. And oh yes, make me rich in the process."

This kind of outlook just wears you and anyone you lead out because there is a level of detail needed to do anything. Your ideas will almost never materialize the way you first conceive them and the better you get at seeing ahead and deciding ahead how you will respond to challenges—big and small—the better poised you will be to succeed.

On the other hand, if you find yourself spinning your wheels on minutiae and never really making progress, it might be time to step back and refocus on the larger context. You might have jumped an important step of deciding in advance what the overall point or outcome of your endeavour is. The endeavour could be anything from a business venture to a board meeting. If you have ever been in a meeting where the conversation got completely derailed leading to a colossal waste of everyone's time and the achievement of nothing, then you know what I'm talking about. Chances are it happened because whoever was responsible either didn't have a clear outcome decided in advance to begin with, or they didn't have an approach to ensure that the goals of the meeting were achieved—they didn't decide in advance how they would respond to unproductive side-tracking.

Meetings are one thing, but this tendency affects if and how bigger decisions are made in many companies as well. It's surprisingly easy to get so caught up in an operational mindset that leaders never revisit the overarching vision.

Companies can employ people and create entire departments to handle these different aspects of the business, should they choose. But when it comes to our personal lives (our health, happiness, and productivity), we need to have that balance within ourselves. There is only so much we can outsource. We need to develop the priceless discipline of deciding in advance both on what the big picture looks like as well as its important details.

KEYS TO DECIDING IN ADVANCE

Deciding in advance is clearly a crucial discipline to develop. But is there an easy model to follow to be able to do it well? I offer you an easy three-step thought process to help. We have already touched on these steps indirectly in the sections before. Here, I will make them more explicit so you can apply them to a broader range of circumstances.

Clarify the goal

It's easy to overcomplicate the concept of goals. But the truth is you are never *not* working on a goal. We are goal-oriented, goal-driven beings. It's impossible to do anything from scratching our noses to setting sail for a new land without some desired outcome—a less itchy nose perhaps, or the promise of a better life. Goals, big and small, direct out actions all the time. In an earlier chapter, we already discussed goals in depth. But there is one more noteworthy use of goals we will add here, one that is not nearly talked about enough. That is the use of goals as filters.

A clearly clarified goal automatically eliminates a lot of options for what is desired, allowed, tolerable, and absolutely unacceptable. A body-builder training for a competition does not have the luxury of eating a lot of the treats we mere mortals indulge in casually and regularly. This person's goals have automatically ruled out bear claws, donuts, and ice-cream until after the competition. But if this person had not clarified the goal of doing well in the competition, well, they would have a harder time with the menu.

The simple act of clarifying your goals can make deciding in advance easier. In fact, it is itself a form of deciding in advance on a future you desire. To make the journey to that future easier, you can decide in advance your route and eliminate detours and dead ends as best you can.

Anticipate scenarios

Ok, you have clarified your goals and you have pictured the better future. Whether it's a grand life-goal like being the head of a multi-national corporation or NGO, or something more immediate like finishing your errands early to spend some time with your family before bed, or something in between like acing an upcoming professional exam. Whatever the case, your goal is clear enough. Now, you need to anticipate scenarios. That is, what are some of the situations that could arise along the way? You won't be able to anticipate everything of course—you're not omniscient. But I'll bet you can anticipate the most likely ones.

This step is often overlooked. If we're being honest, we know that the path to our goals will not be without challenges. But then, for some reason, instead of anticipating those challenges, what do we do? Nothing. We don't even take the time to think about it. I cannot tell you how many goal-setting sessions I have attended where the aspect of anticipating scenarios down the road is not even mentioned, much less addressed. Yet, it's a vital part of success.

When something you have not anticipated happens, it can blindside you, triggering confusion and greatly lowering the chances of responding correctly. You will find it easier to respond effectively to a threat, distraction, or opportunity when you have anticipated it. And while we're talking about responses, let's look at the third step—planning your response.

Plan your response

A Q&A is one of the most stressful parts of any speech for most speakers. It typically comes at the end of the speaker's prepared presentation and, in un-staged presentations, the questions are candid inquiries from audience members. Why is it so stressful for the speaker? It's about control. You see, up to the point of the Q&A, the speaker had been delivering a prepared speech—a polished and well-rehearsed presentation—where they had prior time to think through and synthesize their thoughts coherently. But when the dreaded words "we will now open it up for questions" are uttered, that sense of control is lost. What you have now is a potentially chaotic situation where a single question can throw the speaker off balance and ruin the positive impact of an otherwise successful presentation. What can a speaker do to increase their chances of success? They can decide their responses in advance.

Having clarified the goal of their presentation, they can anticipate likely questions based on the content and context of their presentation, and then prepare their responses in advance. When I coach speakers, this is something I emphasize heavily. The peak-end rule of psychology means that the end of an experience has more influence in shaping how the event is remembered than anything else. And because Q&A sessions happen at the end of a presentation, getting it right is critical.

I get them to walk through their content and develop almost a second layer of content to effectively address questions that might arise from their audience. Essentially, I ask them to decide in advance how they will respond and prepare accordingly. They can then go into the Q&A with a lot more confidence and poise knowing they have lowered the odds of being abashed by a difficult or unexpected question.

You may not be a public speaker, but this principle applies to just about any important activity you are involved in. Life will ask questions of you both literally and metaphorically. Deliberately choosing how you will respond to situations that might arise ahead of them arising will not only make you more able to neutralize threats more efficiently, it will also help you make the most of opportunities—all while maintaining a state of relative confidence and calm. You may not create infinite parallel worlds each time, but you will create a better experience of the one you live in now.

_____

My Goal is to _____ *and if* _____ *happens,*
then I will _____.

_____

CHAPTER 10

The Mindfulness Advantage

If you ever take a trip to the FCJ center in Calgary during summer, and your timing is just right, you might happen upon a curious sight. In a corner of the otherwise bustling downtown area of this vibrant metropolis sits this quaint and quiet retreat facility. The center has a main building complete with private retreat rooms, a library, a chapel, conference space, a kitchen, dining, and lounge area. On the outside are lush green grounds, a community garden, riverside walkways, and a manicured meditation labyrinth. But these won't be what will catch your eye. In fact, you may hardly notice any of this as you pass by. What you will notice, if your timing is right, are a dozen adults walking across the grounds in different directions. In complete silence. And in slow motion. *Super*-slow motion. Every tiny movement measured and deliberate, performed with laser-like focus and concentration.

What you are witnessing is not an open display of choreographed craziness but a very intense exercise in the practice of mindfulness. Those who are familiar with this practice may recognize it as Mindful Walking. It's an integral part of a mindfulness retreat put on by the Center annually where participants go through a mixture of instruction and exercises in mindfulness in the summer months. I guess they do it in summer because it would be difficult to walk mindfully in a Canadian winter. The only thing on your mind in that situation would be, *why the heck would anyone do this to themselves?*

So, summer it is. And people come from all walks of life—from students to working professionals to retirees—all with different reasons for wanting to develop mindfulness. But all recognizing that developing mindfulness is a worthwhile time and financial investment. And they are not alone.

CROSS-LEGGED CEOS

When most people picture a mindfulness teacher or guru, they imagine a skinny, sari-wearing sage with no shoes speaking in mystic prose and koans. But the reality of mindfulness in the 21st century is quite different. Just consider the TLEX® Institute.

This Institute is an international organization delivering mindfulness training for companies all over the world. The company has branches in Asia, Europe, and North America and at the time of this publication, according to the company website, they have delivered training to over 30,000 participants across government, business, corporate, and sports. Their tagline (Mind Management as a Foundation for Well-Being and Agile Leadership), while employing the language of their target market, is clearly about what they offer—mindfulness training. And far from simple saris and esoteric sageliness, the coaches and trainers in the Institute's employ are suit-wearing and business savvy.

The world of business has been turned on to the power of mindfulness. The industry of meditation and mindfulness is now a billion-dollar industry in North America and growing. And with good reason—mindfulness practices, especially meditation, have been proven scientifically to impart amazing benefits.

A MIND FULL OF BENEFITS

In his collection of the profiles of successful people across diverse endeavours, author of *Tools of Titans*, Tim Feriss, says he has found the practice of mindfulness to be the trait most common to all. He interviewed a very diverse group—from hedge fund managers to championship athletes—and in most areas, these high-achievers varied widely. They came from different backgrounds and possessed different sets of skills and talents, as well as varying work habits. But in this one area, there seemed to be the most commonality—most of them practised some form of mindfulness regularly. A commitment to developing mindfulness seemed to be the common success denominator.

I think this is because these people discovered the immense and multi-faceted benefits mindfulness imparts on the body and mind, indeed, in virtually every dimension of wellbeing.

A mindfulness practice has been linked to reduced anxiety, improved cognitive ability (and slowed cognitive decline in old age), lower stress, better sleep, reduced fatigue, pain relief, blood pressure regulation, and an overall feeling of being in a positive mental and spiritual state. All these benefits help make for a better experience of life. But in addition to proven benefits for living a better life, meditation may even help *extend* life, as studies are now indicating that mindfulness practices could have an anti-ageing effect on the body.

In addition, the better we get at mindfulness, the better our self-awareness tends to be as well. We develop an ability to view ourselves and our actions more dispassionately. For many of us, this is just the stepladder we have been missing for levelling up—it gives us the vantage we need to spot destructive, self-sabotaging patterns of thoughts and behaviour. With these insights into ourselves, we can get to work making needed changes to course-correct for success in whatever we are aiming for.

Long story short, if you are looking for one vital discipline that will have a great impact on your life for the better, you can scarcely do better than a mindfulness practice. For this book, we'll focus on how mindfulness practices like meditation help you acquire an important ability, one that is pivotal to your success in whatever endeavour you choose to pursue. And to begin, let's talk a little bit about hormones.

Hormones: Happy, angry, sad...

Hormones are sneaky things. They regulate virtually every aspect of our experience of life while remaining covertly in the background. Importantly, hormones regulate our emotional state; how we *feel* is a function of what hormones are pumping through our veins at the time. Serotonin surging? Well, you feel really good. Dopamine makes you feel dope and adrenaline makes you want to kick butt—literally, being the hormone associated with fight or flight.

The full picture of how hormones affect our emotions is, of course, a large and greatly nuanced subject. There are dozens of hormones regulating many different aspects of our bodies. These hormones also interact in complex ways and are the subject of ongoing research.

For our purposes, we'll concentrate on serotonin, which has established links to many aspects of our physical and emotional states. Most importantly, we will see that meditation alters the body's production of this hormone and, consequently, our state of body and mind in intriguing ways.

Serotonin, confidence, and meditation

The hormone serotonin is associated with the feeling of love and emotional bonding. But while most people are familiar with this aspect of serotonin, there is another important effect serotonin has on us—it's closely linked to feelings of positivity and confidence. In other words, it makes us feel good about ourselves. I'm sure you will agree that feeling good about yourself is a good thing, most of the time. It's ok to feel bad at times—perhaps as a way to acknowledge we have acted badly or negatively out of character— but the healthy use of that is to get us to recompose and get back to a positive frame of mind. It's a place we may visit, not live. A person who spends more time feeling bad about themselves than they do feeling good or neutral would be considered emotionally unhealthy. So, having some positive and self-confidence boosting serotonin flowing is desirable.

Related to this effect of making us feel better about ourselves, serotonin has also been linked to positive mood and high self-efficacy (more on self-efficacy shortly). In fact, most antidepressant medications which aim to improve mood and facilitate positivity work by altering the body's biochemistry so that more serotonin is available to bind to receptors in the brain.

People suffering from depression may benefit from these drugs but, thankfully, you may not need pharmacological interventions to reap the benefits of this hormone. All you may need to do is sit down and breathe.

Enter Zen

In 2010, 15 individuals were led into a dark, sound-proof room in Japan and instructed to sit in straight-backed chairs and breathe from their bellies for half an hour with electrodes and probes stuck on their scalps, temples, shoulder blades, ribs, and behind their ears. The room was in the Department of Physiology in the Toho University of Medicine in Tokyo, and the individuals were volunteers participating in a study of the effects of Zen meditation.

These volunteers were selected based on specific criteria; they had to be healthy with no history of mental, neurological, or respiratory illness. They also had to not be on any medications that could affect brain scan measurements. In addition, they must not have had any prior significant meditation experience in any form. This would help the researchers determine more confidently that any changes that took place during Zen meditation had no interference from other factors. Lastly, of course, they had to be ok with electrodes and probes.

Because the participants were complete novices, before things could get underway, they received brief instruction on breathing patterns for Zen meditation. They were to breathe consciously from the belly with 6-8-second inhales and 9-12-second exhales. The focus of the practice was on the conscious rise and fall of the belly during breathing. It didn't take long for them to master this breathing pattern. They were allowed a few minutes to rest and then it was showtime.

The subjects meditated for 20 minutes while their heart rates, brain activity, and eye movements were measured. Specifically, the researchers wanted to see if there would be any significant changes in brain wave activity and in what areas, if any. They were not disappointed.

The results showed that as little as five minutes into meditating, there was increased brain wave activity in the alpha frequency. This alpha activity has been shown to strongly correlate with a more relaxed state of mind and, importantly, creativity. In the experiment, this increased level of alpha activity was maintained by the participants throughout the 20 minutes. Interestingly, even 30 minutes *after* meditation was done, the alpha activity was still higher than the baseline. Analysis of blood samples collected before and after meditation also showed an increase in blood concentrations of the hormone we have already met—serotonin. This effect also persisted past the end of the meditation session. The participants also reported significant improvement in mood with fewer feelings of depression, anxiety, anger, or confusion. In short, they felt *better*.

The simple act of meditating for just a few minutes had imparted all these benefits —increased creativity, improved mood, more serotonin to fuel positive feelings, and, plausibly, a sense of self-efficacy.

A story of elephants in the savannah

A few weeks before I started writing this book, I was watching a documentary about the African Savannah. If you're looking for a new pastime, you could do much worse than nature documentaries. There is a lot to be learned from them, especially for me—a student of nature, a professional speaker, amateur photographer, and aspiring eclectic traveller. I find myself drawn to well-produced nature documentaries as they push the boundaries of creative storytelling through epic voice narration and immersive cinematography.

In this particular episode, the crew followed a herd of elephants as they struggled to survive the worst drought in over 50 years in the region. The drought lasted many months with some members of the herd dying along the way. But eventually, the rains came. Shortly after, a young male elephant challenged the current leader to a fight for leadership of the herd. Keep in mind the context—they had just been through a terrible drought that claimed the lives of many. The few that survived only barely did. On top of all this, this upstart elephant's chances were literally slim as he was much smaller than the reigning champ. He was also younger and less experienced, but he fought anyway.

African elephants are massive creatures, the largest of all land animals with males weighing up to 6,000kg. These fights produce incredible amounts of force; there is a reason why the old African proverb persists which says that when two elephants fight, it is the grass beneath that suffers the most. To give you an idea of just how violent an elephant fight can be, if you had somehow been able to secure a prime view of the fight seated on the head of one the elephants, you would experience the force of being in a head-on collision between two mid-sized passenger cars...repeatedly. Let's just say you would probably want to have your tusk-belt on.

The fight was gruelling. Again and again, they butted heads. This potentially devastating duel went on for days until eventually, the older male's tusk was shattered and the younger, smaller elephant emerged victorious against the odds.

But what made that underdog elephant go out and fight in the first place? Maybe he knew something about the reigning elephant that the documentary narrator did not—perhaps elephants gossip too. But I suspect it was more to do with a strong biological boost of self-efficacy. And that can tell us a lot about ourselves.

Self-efficacy

Believing in yourself is crucial to winning. Especially if you're playing or fighting against the odds like that young elephant was. It's true for us today, but it was even more crucial in the formative millennia of our species. Before we built buildings, cities, and highways, before we had chain restaurants and one-day shipping of potato chips, we lived in the jungles and plains.

Life was hard back then—we were not so neatly separated from the fierce savagery of the wild. We fought against predators, parasites, and other people all while constantly adapting to the vagaries of the impersonal forces of nature. We had to hunt or gather everything we ate. Today we hunt with mouse drags and clicks and we gather down grocery aisles and manicured orchards. It's easy to forget that as a species, we have survived and even thrived against terribly difficult odds.

In large part, we have survived due to a superior brain. But this brain has had to adapt too, and along the way it acquired some interesting tricks to make us fit for survival. These tricks are called biases—tendencies to perceive ourselves and the world in certain ways which, in turn, predict how we are likely to behave in certain circumstances.

These biases are varied in nature and application—from the negativity bias which makes you pay closer attention to things that may hurt or harm you than things that are positive or neutral, to the social proof bias which makes you use social consensus as a shortcut for decision-making on matters in which you have insufficient information.

But it's the self-efficacy bias which is of interest to us here. This is the adaptation that allows us to believe in ourselves. It also endows us with a sense of agency and the belief in our ability to affect outcomes. This outlook is critical to living a fulfilling life.

As Albert Bandura, Stanford professor of Social Science puts it in his paper aptly titled *Self-Efficacy*:

> Perceived self-efficacy is concerned with people's beliefs in their ability to influence events that affect their lives. This core belief is the foundation of human motivation, performance, accomplishments, and emotional well-being. Unless people believe they can produce desired effects by their actions, they have little incentive to undertake activities or to persevere in the face of difficulties. Whatever other factors may serve as guides and motivators, they are rooted in the core belief that one can make a difference by one's actions.

In her book *Mindset*, Carole Dweck elegantly distilled the research, common sense, and wisdom of the factors for success into two succinct concepts closely related to self-efficacy: Fixed and Growth Mindsets.

The core idea of the book can be summarized as this: People with a fixed mindset do not take on challenges and are not open to improving themselves because they believe that their abilities are, you guessed it, fixed. People with a growth mindset, on the other hand, approach challenges with the willingness to learn and adapt and eventually win because they believe that their abilities can, again, you guessed it, grow.

You could view this in different terms—the people who take on challenges simply believe that they have or can obtain what it takes to win. That is, they have a healthy dose of self-efficacy. The belief leads them to take action in the direction of growth. This is important because we rarely ever start out in possession of everything we need to achieve our goals. But with a healthy dose of self-efficacy mixed with a growth mindset and some action-orientation, you will at least start the journey to attainment, and you cannot arrive without ever setting out.

Back to elephants

It appears that even though self-efficacy is especially crucial in humans, the tendency to be confident, even slightly *over*confident, when it comes to fighting for a resource is a beneficial trait in any species. Indeed, calculated risk-taking in striving for resources—a plausible result of self-efficacy—is observed across many species and is especially common in more intelligent animals.

It's reasonable to surmise that the underdog elephant we met earlier had enough serotonin coursing through his veins to motivate him to take on a bigger and stronger adversary and to eventually win. The underdog cannot win if he does not fight and to fight, he needs to believe in himself—he needs self-efficacy.

In this chapter, I have dwelt quite a bit on the different aspects of self-efficacy. This is because, as was mentioned earlier, it is key to success. But how does it all tie in with serotonin and meditation?

Meditation acts on your brain to trigger the release of serotonin. Serotonin makes you feel good about yourself and over time, improves your outlook. It helps reduce and regulate negative emotions and boosts your confidence. Feeling good about yourself and having a positive outlook are critical aspects of your mindset and self-efficacy, which determine how likely you are to confidently pursue your goals and dreams. When you do pursue your dreams, meditation also increases your likelihood to come up with creative solutions to problems by stimulating the alpha brainwaves we encountered in the Zen experiment. As you solve problems and build confidence, a positive feedback loop is created, and a virtuous cycle of self-fulfilling prophecy is launched. Momentum builds so that you, with your improved self-efficacy, continue to grow and learn and change who you are to become the type of person who can do what you want to do. As the famous quote goes, "the people who are crazy enough to think they can change the world, are the ones who do."

Many of us are not born with this level of confidence, but through the development and application of mindfulness practices, we can gain deep insight into ourselves and build the power to change who we are for the better.

HOW TO DEVELOP MINDFULNESS

The character of mindfulness comes from a practice of mindfulness, just like any other character. We become disciplined by practicing discipline. We become skillful by practicing our skill. We become mindful by practicing mindfulness. Practicing works best when it is systematic and deliberate, and when it comes to mindfulness, it can take many different forms.

Not only is there walking meditation as we have seen, but there is also meditative reading, Zen meditation, Transcendental Meditation (TM), visualization, certain forms of prayer, contemplation, body scanning, and autogenic training. Not to mention physical exercises like Tai Chi, Qigong, and the ubiquitous Yoga. The number of options can quickly become bewildering.

But what matters more than what kind of practice you choose is that you practice *consistently*. Don't expect to be totally transformed after a few minutes of meditation. The benefits that accrue from meditation do just that, they accrue. The good news is that although the most benefit is gained with prolonged practice, every time you enter a state of mindfulness, you reap benefits.

It's best to practice daily, but even a few times a week can be beneficial. Better to choose a frequency with which you can be consistent. To help you with that, see the principles of deciding in advance covered in chapter 9. In brief, choose and uphold a fixed time and place for your practice. Anticipate any scenarios that may hinder you and have a plan for how to evade, overcome or remedy them.

Scheduling a meditation practice first thing in the morning or the last thing at night will work for most people because these are also usually the quietest times both physically and mentally. These times have the added benefit of setting the tone for your day on one hand and helping purge your thoughts before going to bed on the other.

That said, it also helps to intersperse your day with mini-mindfulness moments where you can. As little as two minutes of deliberate mindfulness through breathing exercises (more on this next) will boost your sense of wellbeing. And as we saw with the research from Toho, going up to five minutes could get some fantastic bio-alchemy going for your body and mind.

Starter mindfulness exercise

While I do not hold any one technique as being objectively better than another, in the spirit of this book, I offer three vital elements that show up again and again in most mindfulness practices. Getting better at these will help you with whatever practice you choose. They are the ability to:

- **control your attention**
- **control your breath** and
- **relax your muscles** at will.

All three are closely related and can be strengthened at once using a straightforward mindfulness exercise.

The exercise

Sit in a chair in a comfortable position with your spine erect. You want to be in a physical state of relaxed alertness. No slouching, but also avoid being tense or rigid. You want your weight neither tipping forward nor back but going straight down into the chair and floor. You may also sit on a mat on the floor but this is not necessary. I know the lotus position looks cool and super-spiritual, but it also requires a high degree of flexibility that few possess. Better to be comfortable because the distraction of any physical discomfort turns this from a mindfulness practice to a pain tolerance test. So, choose a comfortable position; a straight-back chair works fine—simple and effective.

Next, begin to breathe deeply with at least a few seconds for both your inhale and exhale, holding briefly after each inhale for a second or two before exhaling. Fill your lungs up completely with each inhale breathing in through the nose, empty them out completely with each exhale, breathing out through the mouth. Focus your attention on the sensation of breathing—the rise and fall of your chest or stomach and the coolness of the air through your nostrils.

As you do this, let your muscles relax completely. From the crown of your head through your eyelids, your face and down to your toes...relax.

Keep your attention focused on your breath. You may want to close your eyes as this eliminates any distracting visual stimuli. If you find your attention wandering, don't fret. Just bring it back while maintaining your breath. Continue this focussed and relaxed breathing pattern over the course of a few minutes (five to seven minutes is a decent start if you are completely new to this). At the end of the exercise, just sit quietly for a few more seconds then slowly open your eyes.

You can start with just a few minutes and over time increase how long you spend. What is more important than how long you spend is how well the time is spent—quality over quantity. Give it your full commitment for however long you decide. Doing so will ensure you get the most benefit.

Focused attention, mindful breathing, and relaxation form a solid foundation for any mindfulness practice, and this simple exercise will help you build these abilities. In fact, if this exercise was all you practiced diligently, you would still benefit immensely and begin to enjoy the multifaceted gains that come from the vital discipline of mindfulness.

As you get better though, you can start to layer on some more involved techniques such as replacing the focus on the breath with a visualization or a focus on certain positive feelings like compassion, love, or gratitude. You may opt instead to engage in some quiet prayer or contemplation or you may decide to explore the sensations of your body or the state of your emotions. There are so many possible places to go from here with the different forms of mindfulness practice. Once you get a rhythm going, you can have a lot of fun with it and sample the different genres to find which fits best for you.

Getting started is the hard part and if you're having challenges in initiating the habit, there are many useful apps these days that can help you develop and sustain a mindfulness practice. A search in the app store for the terms *meditation* or *mindfulness* will yield results you can sift through and pick from. A lot of these apps have free versions you can get started with. As you build up your practice, you can decide whether upgrading to a paid plan makes sense for you or not.

However you decide to start or practice, you will find that through regular exercise, your skills in mindfulness will improve by the day. And having developed to a significant degree, you might also be pleasantly surprised to notice that—on top of the positive impacts to your self-efficacy and health—mindfulness enhances other vital areas of your life too.

CHAPTER 11

The Planning Animal

One of my clearest memories from childhood was a rather irritating elementary science class. I must have been around eight years old sitting in the classroom absolutely outraged at a claim the science teacher had made. He had dared to suggest that human beings—me, my family, my friends, *all* of us—were animals. How dare he?! To my mind, animals were things like cats, dogs, sheep, snails, and cows. I found the statement insulting, as did many of the other kids in the class. We didn't care about the teacher's logical arguments drawing parallels in physiology and inviting us to compare ourselves to other species. His logic just couldn't click. Even though I had a lot in common with the other animals around me—two eyes, two ears, one mouth, etc.—I thought myself too advanced to be *just an animal*. I believe this repulsion is natural for most people. Despite all the evidence which points directly to this aspect of our nature, there is still a natural resistance to fully embracing the narrative that we are animals.

Well, elementary science was a long time ago and, thankfully, I have learned a lot since then. For one, the word "animal" no longer carries a negative connotation. Today, I'm not offended at the suggestion that me or my kind are animals. But even though as humans we share quite a lot in common with other species, we are remarkably different in key areas. These differences can sometimes be so obvious as to appear banal; the fact that we walk on two legs, wear clothing, live in condos, celebrate birthdays, paint, play music (and PlayStation), text, tweet, read, and write, are all clear distinguishing factors, evidences if you like, of our superiority or at least uniqueness from other species. But all the things that make us distinctly human, though numerous on the surface, are actually traceable to a few vital abilities we have been endowed with. In fact, if you asked a biologist what makes us so different from the other wonderful creatures we share this world with, they would say, well, a lot and a little.

You see, physiologically, we are very similar to other creatures, particularly other mammals. Popular science has pretty much desensitized us to our similarities to the great apes, as have visits to the zoo for me personally. There is something eerily familiar when you look into the eyes of a chimpanzee or gorilla. So, for the most part, we take our similarity to great apes for granted. But it surprised me to learn of how similar we are to less majestic mammals.

Take the bat for example. This small, flying, nocturnal, winged mammal appears as dissimilar to us as can be. But the difference is skin-deep. The bat skeleton is unsettlingly similar to the human one. Take a human skeleton, exaggerate the phalanges, reshape the facial bones a touch here and there and shrink its overall size and you pretty much have the same structure. The Museo del Desierto (Desert Museum) in Mexico actually has a display comparing an enlarged bat skeleton to a human one—the resemblance is striking.

Biologists refer to this as "homology"—the phenomenon in which structures or genes are shared by animals (like humans and bats) that do not belong to the same group. This phenomenon is surprisingly common. In fact, we humans share a lot of our DNA with other animals with, among others, about a 90% match to domestic cats. That would explain my propensity for long naps. In this sense, compared to other animals, we differ only a little.

The big differentiator sits in our skulls—our brains. Our brains are quite large, weighing about 3lbs (or 1.4kg). But size isn't all there is to it. If it were, then elephants would reign supreme. At 11lbs (5kg) or about three and a half times the size of the human brain, elephants have the largest brains of any land mammal.

If brain size were all that counts, the two elephants we talked about earlier would have been too busy unravelling the mysteries of existence to be getting into brawls. It would also mean that the orangutan would be an utter dunce with its mere 370g or 13ounces of brain. Instead, it turns out to be a rather clever ape, as far as apes go.

No, it's not just the fact that our brains are large, it's the incredibly complex nature of our brains and the components they possess that make all the difference. These are what impart onto us what scientists call "higher functions" like memory, communication, and thinking. If there was one vital factor that makes us humans different from other animals, it would be our brains. These brains make us very special and more cognitively advanced, as far as we can tell, than other creatures. As for when, how, or even why our brains developed to this degree, the scientific community is not certain. What is evident though is that our brains impart to us some unique and immensely useful abilities that other creatures seem to lack. Specifically, language and, very importantly, *imagination*. In this sense, compared to other animals, we differ a lot!

As far as scientists can tell, we're neither the first nor the only creatures to develop a means of communication. Dolphins rely heavily on sound to communicate effectively and some species of monkeys can vocalize fairly nuanced messages to each other, distinguishing between different types of predators, for example.

Most species, however, seem to have rather fixed language patterns—set pieces or phrases if you will. In other words, their "languages" do not recombine easily to relay new thoughts or ideas. If we think about language as mental machinery, you could say they don't have enough modules, hinges, or moving parts. You might argue that post-internet culture teenage humans are the same and as much as I would like to agree, even they are significantly more sophisticated. The fact is that when it comes to nuance and complexity as well as fluidity in language, none come close to us humans.

What this means is that we can communicate huge amounts of information with a great amount of detail. And the ability to combine and reconfigure language means that we can give birth to new concepts and possibilities and, perhaps more importantly, articulate them to others who can then do the same. And on and on it goes till a civilization is formed and routinely transformed. As Steven Pinker remarks in his book, *The Language Instinct*: "Simply by making noises with our mouths, we can reliably cause precise new combinations of ideas to arise in each other's minds."

Just think of all the thoughts and ideas that have trickled through thousands of years. From the survival-driven cautionary warnings to the accretion of scientific, philosophical, and religious thought that have shaped how we live today. It's clear that our facility for language, gifted to us through the sophistication of our brains, has made an incalculable difference in how well we have fared on earth.

But the brain not only gives us the ability to represent reality through language, it also gives us the ability to *imagine* new realities. We can make things up and, more importantly, we can think not only in real-time but *through* time as well. As a result, we can anticipate possible future occurrences and our responses to them in a highly adaptive and flexible way. This is easy to take for granted until we explore its implications and the fact that while other animals seem to be able to do this to an extent, none as far as we know can do it as well as us. And this is one of the vital differentiators of our species.

CPA: CHIEF PLANNING ANIMAL

Ants anticipate winter and either stockpile food that they then consume in the cold months, or eat more during fall to accumulate fat and then hibernate during winter. Bears binge exclusively, not even bothering to save for the snowy days but opting instead to sleep through them. Other examples of animal migration, hiding, hoarding, and nesting behaviours abound, all of which suggest that other animals have the ability to execute plans.

Wasps and their nest-building abilities are an interesting example here. Wasps build nests to serve reproductive, protective, and, in some species, social functions—not that different from us really. And also, like human nests, wasp nests are amazing feats of construction—incredibly complex when built collectively, often with millions of cells per nest.

Mud wasps, as their name implies, build their edifices using mud. Other species construct theirs by collecting and mixing plant fibres with their saliva to produce a paper-like material which they fashion into different structures and cells in the nest. In the case of the mud wasp, these nests are constructed by using mud to line the inner walls of an excavated hole in the ground. The wasp follows this up by painstakingly assembling an elaborate mud funnel from mud pellets which is specially constructed to make it difficult for parasitic wasps and other insects to enter. She then lays her eggs and provisions the nest with tasty caterpillar treats appropriately sealed in individual cells in the nest for her unborn spawn to enjoy when it hatches. Finally, the wasp seals the nest entrance with a plug of mud and destroys the funnel. Job done.

The degree of self-organization required to accomplish such a feat is so remarkable that several computer scientists have used the process as inspiration for the development of computational models. Researchers in the University of Calgary's Computer Science Department, for example, used the wasp's nest-building behavioural mechanism as inspiration for developing a construction algorithm.

On the surface, these applications appear to be an acknowledgement of the intelligence of these insects. But this is actually a clue to how fundamentally codified their behaviour is, as was demonstrated in a revealing, albeit rather impish, series of experiments conducted at the Zoology Department of the University of Sydney Australia.

In the experiments, researchers caused selected mud wasps quite a bit of grief and consternation by tinkering with their mud-nest construction project—stealing entire entrance funnels, burying parts of the nest, downright poking holes in the walls, that sort of thing. But it was not all for fun and giggles, the researchers wanted to see how the wasps would respond. They believed this would reveal the underlying processes governing how this tiny insect could execute such a complex task. What they observed provided some interesting insights.

If a structure such as a funnel (one of the more involved structures to complete as we have seen) was suddenly gone after the wasp returned to the nest (having been stolen by the prankish scientists), the wasp didn't launch an investigation. It simply built a new one as if it hadn't built one before. The wasp acted similarly when it noticed holes made by the scientists in its absence—it simply patched them up and moved on.

But the researchers did not only steal or break things, they also *added* structures that the wasp did not. For example, the researchers installed a funnel in a nest that did not yet have one while the winged builder was away. When the wasp arrived to this glaring home upgrade it had not made, it didn't seem phased. It simply inspected the funnel briefly and then continued building as though it was her who had put the funnel there in the first place.

That would be as if you came home from work one summer evening and right there where there was nothing but grass in your yard when you left in the morning there was a brand-new gazebo complete with outdoor chairs and a state-of-the-art gas-powered barbeque grill. And instead of wondering what the dickens was going on, you changed into your favourite floral print t-shirt, called your besties over, threw a few drinks in the igloo cooler, and fired up the grill.

These results, the researchers said, indicate that the wasps seemingly intelligent behaviour is really an inflexible, hard-wired set of responses to environmental cues. As they put it:

> Nest construction occurs as a stimulus response chain sequence of events in which the completion of one stage provides the stimulus for commencement of the next.

So, even though one could refer to the behaviours of certain animals like ants and bears and wasps as planning, they are not at the level of sophistication that really counts, and scientists have shown they do not fulfill the cognitive conditions for true planning. Even where some of these cognitive abilities appear to exist, they come nowhere near humans in the span, complexity, and reach, with the most advanced apes operating at the level of a human toddler at best.

Similar to the language abilities discussed earlier, most animal planning abilities lack the scope, complexity, and flexibility conferred graciously upon man. We reflect and we also project; we have hindsight and we have foresight; we can think in creative and analytical ways in either direction—past or future.

How far into the future? Well consider that, on the religious front, most organized religions speak of an afterlife, projecting many, many years into the future. Sometimes, all the way into eternity. That's about as far as you can go. And on the purely secular front, scientists are engaged in serious debates about how our planet began billions of years ago and, perhaps more interestingly, how our entire universe—of which our planet is but a mere speck—will end *trillions* of years in the future. Will it be a big crunch when everything collapses back into itself, or a big rip as the expansion of the universe careens out of control? Will it even end at all? Who knows for sure?

The point is not the answer to these profound and perplexing questions. The point is that our ability to think this far ahead is a uniquely human trait—one that, coupled with our other distinctive human cognitive abilities, can serve us immensely. It allows us to use our imaginations to anticipate events that have not yet happened, and then *plan* for them.

Of course, the fact that we are capable of planning does not guarantee that we will practice planning. But not using this ability is to forego one of the Vital Few powers of being human. Going through life without using your God-given power to plan is like going through an arts and craft project without using your thumbs. Sure, you could probably do it, but you might not enjoy yourself very much, and what you produce will be far less than you were capable of.[7]

A PLANNING PRIMER

Perhaps the single greatest challenge we face when it comes to planning is the act itself. Our failings in planning are usually not in *how* to plan but in *if* we plan. Even the person of the most modest education and meagre intelligence, if armed with the necessary information, can put together a simple step-by-step process of how to get a thing done—most planning is commonsensical. However, the act itself is mentally demanding.

So, many shun it, opting instead to "take the jump and build their wings on the way down"—an expression I have always cringed at every time I hear it uttered. Usually, because it is spoken in the context of a project that already has the hallmarks of a disaster waiting to be signed off on. Other times, it's a lazy side-step—a manifestation of an aversion to work or conflict. In any case, it is not a strategy, at least not a wise one.

Another common rebuttal is: "Why plan if we know the plans are going to change anyway? Let's just go with it." To which

---

[7] Your two thumbs are 20% of your phalanges but you depend on them in virtually 100% of all tasks you complete using tools with your hands. The two grips you depend on—the precision grip and the power grip—depend heavily on the use of your thumbs.

the answer is that the act of planning is valuable in and of itself because it forces you to a level of clarity that is hard to gain otherwise. When you make a plan, you come face to face with gaps in your own thinking, and the process of filling those gaps—if only to make your plan coherent—makes your thoughts coherent as well. You are that much sharper and more confident when you have taken time to plan a course of action for something, whether it be an activity, project, career, or a life.

That we should plan is obvious, but whether or not we actually take the pains to do so is another matter entirely. Yet, to employ one of the most famous quotes on the subject: When you fail to plan, you plan to fail.

Planning, as a discipline, is indispensable in your journey to living at the center of your Vital Few. Depending on how far you are from this center now, perhaps a *lot* of planning will be needed.

This planning primer will be short and to the point. We have already hinted at planning in Book I: Chapter 7 where we deconstructed goal-setting, and again in Book II: Chapter 9 where we discussed deciding in advance. Here, we will bring the ideas together starting with a thought-experiment to engage your vital human powers of imagination and thinking through time; and then concretizing it into an initial roadmap that addresses the five questions every good plan must answer. We will use the example of a plan to create an ideal life, but this can be used for any project or undertaking complex enough to require organized action.

Step 1: Begin at the end

Beginning with the end-goal in mind—an ideal life—get to work clarifying the successful outcome as best you can. Imagine as much relevant detail as possible. Clarify the important aspects of your life (the Wheel of Life from Chapter 7 might prove useful). Take each segment and draft what your experience is in that area. How much money are you earning? How many hours a week do you have for leisure or to spend with family? How are you learning and growing as a person?

It wouldn't hurt to describe how you are doing most of your work in the realm of your Vital Few and how that has translated positively into other aspects.

For a project other than your ideal life, you can use the metrics that measure success as your criteria; a business-related plan may use key performance indicators (KPIs), for example.

Step 2: Backwards design

With the end defined at high resolution, you will now ask yourself the all-important question: How did I get there?

Notice the question is not how *will I* get there. This is important. "How did I get there?" triggers your creativity in a profound way. The answer to it is your action plan in embryonic form, and it needs to address five key questions:

- ❑ What happened?
- ❑ When did it happen?
- ❑ Who did it (or got it done)?
- ❑ How did they (or I) do it?
- ❑ Why was it important?

By working backwards from the end, you are leveraging foresight and, notably, hindsight as a way to gain insights and reveals gaps. Filling the revealed gaps and moving forward on the uncovered action steps will start the pull in the direction of the realization of your ends.

It is worthy of note that these five questions will likely each have multiple answers and they may not line up neatly and chronologically. But part of planning is making sense out of the information this exercise produces.

Step 3: Action planning

Lay out all the information you have generated and organize it into an order that works forwards in time—essentially, an order you can take action on. Use a format that appeals to you. A simple bulleted list can work; so can a table or a chart. What matters is that the layout appeals to your preferred way of organizing and processing information.

Once arranged in a forward direction through time, you can get to work on the first thing within your power to tackle. It could be as simple as a phone call to a business contact to schedule a coffee-chat or a web search for some information. What matters is that it is *actionable*.

Step 4: Work (and rework) the plan

Without action, even the prettiest and most detailed plans are not much good. A simple (even an oversimplified) plan that is executed and refined over time will yield infinitely more returns than one that is left gathering dust in a drawer. If you don't work your plan, your plan can't work for you.

That said, the quality of your plans depends heavily on the quality of the information you are working with. Therefore, it would be wise to include in your plans the commitment to finding and filling your own knowledge gaps and checking your blind spots.

This is more an approach to planning and the execution of plans than a step in the planning process—a philosophy, if you will. One that keeps us alert to the opportunities to refine and redefine our plans and approaches as new and better information comes to our awareness—information we actively seek out in the course of planning and executing.

With this information, we can revisit and rework our plans, tweaking where needed and overhauling if required, but never losing sight of the end we are after.

Hopefully, by now you are convinced of the value of planning as a vital discipline, and have in your possession a straightforward framework to exercise it. If you have decided to engage this Homo sapien super-power of planning, you will benefit from being aware that our machinery for planning, while being superior to other animals, is not without its glitches.

A CURIOUS QUIRK

There is a quirk of the human mind that is at once a source of great strength, and a stumbling block. We have explored one side of this trait already in chapter 10 when we discussed self-efficacy. But self-efficacy is only a part of a larger bias system running in our wetware—what psychologists call the "optimism bias". Plainly put, the optimism bias causes us to *overestimate* our own abilities and *underestimate* challenges. And while this sounds more like a glitch in the system than a selling feature, there is benefit in it.

If, looking within, we didn't believe in our abilities to achieve a goal, we would likely never pursue it and so never make progress. Fixating on the fact that we don't possess all the attributes, skills, or resources needed to succeed at the outset of a venture would stop us from ever venturing. Sometimes, we're better off just to get going and learn along the way—fill in the gaps as it were—a la Dweck's growth mindset.

Also, looking outside ourselves, if we waited until every minute detail and every permutation was worked out, it would take forever to start or finish any project, from pursuing a degree to starting a business to even planning a vacation. The world is just too complex for that and we would end up in an ossified state of analysis paralysis. There are too many variables to contend with most of the time, especially where other sentient beings with their own aims, faults, and motivations are involved. Again, we are better off starting with as much as we know and deciding in advance to the best of our abilities, and then adjusting as needed.

So, the optimism bias does have its usefulness. The problem arises when this psychological system—which is meant to spur us on—ends up blinding us to realities that would frustrate our loftiest intentions. Or worse, causes us to ignore these realities in a belief that either these things wouldn't happen to *us,* or that things will work out...*somehow.*

It is this dubious side of our knack for optimism that we will consider here. And we will do so by exploring its two sides—our overestimation of ourselves, and our underestimation of challenges.

Let us begin with the question: How long does it take to write a graduate thesis?

The Planning Fallacy

In 1994, researchers in Canada asked 37 college students enrolled in their final semester of an Honours Thesis program the question: How long will it take to write your graduate thesis?

The researchers did this as part of their investigation into a previously proposed phenomenon called the "planning fallacy".

The planning fallacy was first introduced by Daniel Kahneman and his research partner Amos Tversky in their studies in decision-making. At the center of the theory is the claim that people, left unaided, will almost certainly underestimate how long it will take them to complete a task—this being a manifestation of our *over*estimation of our abilities.

So, for this group of college students, the question the researchers wanted to answer was straightforward enough—would the students underestimate how long it will take them to complete their thesis?

To make things more interesting though, the researchers threw in a twist. They had the college students predict how long it would take to complete their thesis under two different and aptly termed conditions:

- The optimistic condition: If everything went as well as it possibly could, and
- The pessimistic condition: If everything went as poorly as it possibly could.

In other words, they were blatantly asking the college students to be optimistic on one hand and pessimistic on the other, to see if it would have an impact on their predictions. They then followed the students to see how long it actually took them to write their thesis.

On average, the students predicted approximately a 34-day completion time. In reality, they actually took an average of 55.5 days. But how did the hypothetical conditions affect the predictions?

The optimistic predictions averaged out at a truly rose-tinted 27.4 days, while the pessimistic predictions came in at 46 days. Even at their most pessimistic, the students' predictions still fell short. But at least by taking the pessimistic outlook, they were much closer to reality than when they were thinking optimistically.

What the researchers observed was a classic case of the planning fallacy at work. But on top of that, these results indicate that, contrary to popular opinion, pessimism can be a virtue. At least when it comes to planning how long it will take to get something done, you are better off assuming the worst than the best—you stand a better chance of being closer to reality that way. As a general rule, always assume tasks and projects will take longer than seems reasonable to you.

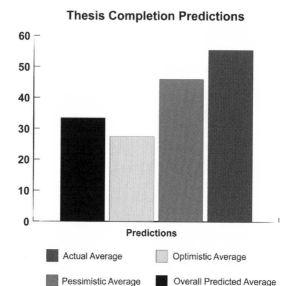

Figure: Thesis Completion Rates: Predicted vs Actual

Even professional estimators do this. An audience member from one of my seminars on planning once came up to me and shared how the planning fallacy played into his world of estimating cost and timelines for multi-million-dollar projects. He explained the exacting and rigorous scientific formula employed by estimators all over the world for estimating and quoting on projects—big, small and everything in-between.

Pay attention now, here it is: If you are sure you know what you are doing, double the quote; if you are kind of sure, triple it; if you have never done this kind of work before, quadruple it.

It was so complicated, he joked as he handed me a sheet of paper, that he had written it down for me on the back of my seminar feedback form so that I don't forget its intricate details. That was my belly-laugh for the day.

The lesson from both the planning fallacy and my delightful audience member is that overestimating your abilities is a real and present threat to the success of your plans. In general, it is best to be open to learning and receiving the counsel of people with more skill and experience than you. Even when you are working in your Vital Few areas of strength, you don't have 360-degree vision or infinite perspective. As much as possible, make provisions in your plans to shore up your weaknesses. And of course, always double how long you think it will take you to get a task done, at least.

The Perfect World Delusion

Now that we have seen that overestimating our abilities can trip us up, let's turn to the other side of the optimism bias—the underestimation of challenges. Or what I call the Perfect World Delusion.

In a perfect world, your plans would unfold without a hitch. You would complete every task exactly when you intended, and so would everyone else your plans depended on—clients, colleagues, contractors, to name a few, would all work in perfect step, not missing a single beat, to the achievement of your goals. And not just them. Your friends and family too, and indeed all of creation—from the weather to the city transit system—would conspire to bring you swimmingly to your goals exactly as you intended and at the precise place and time you foresaw. In a perfect world, everything you planned would go perfectly.

But of course, that is a delusion. The problem is a lot of our plans are based on this impractically optimistic outlook—the Perfect World Delusion.

While looking through the cloud of the Perfect World Delusion, it's really hard to see ahead of us, not to mention being able to anticipate the projectiles that may fly in from left field. Otherwise viable businesses have been shut down, New Year resolutions have crumbled, and corporate and individual goals have been frustrated simply because of this Perfect World Delusion. The people involved expected everything to go smoothly from point A to point B *every time*. And when things did not, it was devastating and demoralizing.

The entrepreneur did not anticipate slow and difficult days or pushback on pricing or financing. The fitness lifestyle resolutioneer did not anticipate an increased workload taking away time available for exercise. The company did not anticipate their sales declining, and the goal-maker did not anticipate the roadblocks that hinder the execution of their plans.

The reality is that things *will* go wrong, possibly in a myriad of ways. Things can go wrong as a result of a miscalculation on your part while creating your plans; maybe you overestimated the demand for your product or misjudged how high a price the market could bear. On the other hand, things can go wrong in an impersonal, life-happens kind of way; the flight being delayed, changes to government regulations, you (or the person you depended on to get something done) catching a cold, etc. These are the kind of events that could happen no matter how well-informed your plans were.

The reason most people avoid confronting potential challenges is that, frankly, it's not a lot of fun. But it can be if approached with the right attitude. If it is done in the mindset that we possess or can obtain what we need to overcome those challenges, then we can treat it as a game of wits. In fact, anticipating that challenges will arise and that it is just part of the game has the effect of supplying the grit and resilience we need to push through—we know that victory is waiting patiently on the other side of the trial.

The greater part of your superiority as a human over the other creatures with whom we share this planet lies in your powers of imagination, and your ability to think through time. These not only allow you to imagine a new and better reality for yourself in the future, but they also empower you to make plans and anticipate potential disruptions to those plans. Whether your goals are confronted by a personal or an impersonal force, your best bet against the Perfect World Delusion—the belief that your aims will go unchallenged—is never to buy into it in the first place.

Make the most of your human superpower by making your plans as robust as possible, balancing your healthy self-efficacy with a dose of pessimism to make sure you cover all the bases and give yourself the best chance of success. All that said, do not be overly rigid with your plans. New knowledge will come your way, so use it to enhance yourself and refine your approach. You will have a smoother journey and arrive at your destination quicker and easier this way.

CHAPTER 12

Learning the TVF Way

I have read a hundred things in Livy that another has not, or not taken notice of at least; and Plutarch has read a hundred more there than ever I could find, or than, peradventure, that author ever wrote.
Michel de Montaigne

Let me start by saying plainly that you do not need to master everything you do. For some things, good enough is, well, good enough. The principles of learning (in this chapter) and of Deliberate Practice (in the next chapter) will help you simply get better—no matter how *much* better you want to get. The principles will also provide you with a more methodical approach to your learning and practice that will save you time and effort in the long run.

That said, once you have identified your Vital Few skills, especially those that fall into your TVF Sweet Spot, you will benefit from mastering them. This is the secret of taking your Vital Few to their maximum potential. Good enough is good enough for many things, but it's best to aim for mastery in your Vital Few.

A LEARNING PRACTICE

I have a friend who describes learning as his affliction. His goal is to add a new body of knowledge to himself every year. Sometimes, it's a formal professional certification and other times, it's a pre-meditated study of selected books on specific topics. Watching his career flourish from the outside, many peers have expressed surprise at how quickly he has risen. Those of us with inside knowledge, on the other hand, have wondered why it has taken so long. He calls this an affliction; I call it a healthy learning practice.

We've already talked about developing a mindfulness practice and how that practice provides immense psychological and physiological benefits. Here we talk about the need to develop a learning practice. That is, a systemized, routinized approach to learning.

Aim to never be without some interesting topic or subject of study.

Our ability to learn so effectively is also another benefit of our immensely complex and malleable brains. And that's good because often the gap between where we are and where we want to be, is a learning gap. Filling these gaps can bring us closer to our ideal, faster. Aside from the enjoyment learning can provide, a new piece of information can save us months, even years of toil and labour. Learning a new skill can catapult your career, or at least save you from obsolescence. And improving our attitudes and mindsets is an ever-continuing personal development pursuit. In this era of rapid change, learning is no longer a luxury.

Therefore, it's no surprise that as you begin to live a life based on your Vital Few, you might find that you want to get better at a few things you've identified using your Vital Venn and TVF Matrix. Getting better will mean learning, and because of this, personal development and learning are at the core of TVF living.

Sadly, the bad experiences a lot of people have had with a poor school system has left a bad taste in their mouths. If that has been your experience, I invite you to separate the concept of "school" from "learning". You can redefine your learning experience and start to enjoy it—especially once you've seen how much benefit it can bring you. A big part of this is developing more efficient learning techniques to help you master your Vital Few quicker. Let's discuss how you may approach learning differently to ensure you are spending the least effort and gaining the most value.

ECONOMICAL LEARNING

There has never been more of a demand on you to acquire new skills and update (or replace) old established ones than now. There has never been more rapid obsolescence of skills (and people) in the history of our civilizations. However, likewise, there has never been easier access to information. Never have there been more rewards either for being a highly-skilled "knowledge worker". Put these together and you can see that the same circumstances that spell extinction for the person who refuses to adopt a continuous learning approach to work and life also spell success to the one who does.

The dictionary defines the word "economical" as "giving good value or service in relation to the amount of money, time, or effort spent". A good definition no doubt, but I define it plainly as "using no more than is necessary". When you use more than is necessary, you end up with waste, and waste is costly.

Economical Learning refers to the method of studying with minimal waste of time and energy as a result of a clear intention and result-oriented engagement with information. When you adopt this approach to learning, you will easily multiply your effectiveness as much by what you do, as by what you don't waste your time doing.

The method is broken down into three distinct stages:

- The reverse epiphany
- Pre-determination and deliberation
- Pre-study Priming (PSP)

Step one: The reverse epiphany

Before you ever pick up a book or look at a course, you must experience the reverse epiphany. This step is just as important as the act of studying because it sets the stage for everything else that follows.

This is the stage where you come to a realization that you have a knowledge or skill gap. The old saying goes, *you don't know what you don't know.* While this is mostly true, by the end of this stage you will at least know that you need to know. Better still, you will know *what* you need to know.

The potholes in your path

The pothole is a good metaphor to describe the gaps of knowledge and skill that riddle the path to success, much like potholes on a decrepit road.

Some of these knowledge gaps are so large they are more like craters, such as the one you would experience when trying to make a huge career change or shift into a new field. Others you could probably drive right over at moderate speed with nothing but a little discomfort as you pass, such as putting together a piece of furniture from IKEA. Frustrating, I know, but you probably don't need to take time off work to enroll in a weekend boot camp to assemble your new curiously-named floating shelf.

Economical learning means that you give no more or less attention and energy to a pothole than is necessary to successfully pass it with no damage to your vehicle, and minimal impact on your speed.

Start with duh

In his best-selling book, *Start with Why*, Simon Sinek describes the importance for leaders to clarify and communicate their motivation for doing what they do—what he calls their "why". This, he says, will help them connect and engage with the people they lead and drive their vision forward. Here I would add that, having found your "why"—your deep-seated drive for pursuing what you are after—the next thing to find is your *duh!* That is, where you lack knowledge or skill.

Your duh is important because it can frustrate your why if it's not addressed. Passion and vision alone can't get you there, you also need information to solve problems and overcome obstacles. If you don't recognize that you lack knowledge or skill, you may exhaust yourself hurling large boulders of time and energy at a problem that could be solved with a small nugget of insight, or a slight tweak in technique.

Step two: Pre-determination and deliberation

For a lot of people, once they identify, albeit in fuzzy terms, what knowledge or skill they lack, they jump online inserting keywords into search engines, browsing books, courses, and program brochures.

However, there is a problem with this approach—it lacks deliberation. And deliberation on your learning, especially the desired outcomes, is crucial to Economical Learning.

Have you ever passed through a course or read a book that was meant to prepare you for a career or impart some skill for a specific role or job function only for you to start the job and have to re-learn it all over again?

What happened? Was the course bad? Maybe. Was the instructor uninteresting? Perhaps. But my money is on the fact that you were not crystal clear about what you were going to get out of the course or book. You shot your energy in many different directions, probably making decent grades or getting the overall gist of the material but not coming away with any tangible improvements in ability. As a result, you were like a kid with a water gun instead of a trained sniper.

It's the ability to attain a clear focus on your desired outcome that is at the core of any successful learning experience. And this is what the predetermination step is all about. It involves thoughtfully outlining exactly what you need to glean from any learning effort you embark on. Without this, you will find yourself wandering through the content with no real takeaway simply because you didn't pre-set the goal. Conversely, pre-setting the goal makes you much more effective and focused.

For example, whenever I am called upon to deliver a keynote, I will do a lot of new reading and re-reading in line with the theme of the client's event. I have my general theme of expertise, but to ensure the presentation is tailored and impactful, I read specific material. By clearly predetermining the purpose of my study—be it identifying industry trends, extracting relevant statistics or quotes, mining relevant inspirational stories, etc.—I am *much* more focused during my study and can quickly qualify (and disqualify) certain books or certain chapters of books and courses. In other words, I am extremely clear about what I am fishing for. It also helps me to quickly recognize it when I see it and document it for later review.

You can try this approach for yourself. Predetermine what you need to gain from a study effort guided by your reverse epiphany, and ask questions of the information you interact with. Good questions produce good answers.

Critical questions

When I worked as a Learning Strategist and an Instructional Designer, and even today when clients engage with me to train or coach their staff, one of the vital questions I ensure I have nothing less than absolute clarity on is: What do you want the learner to be able to do?

The simplicity of this question may surprise you. If so, you will be even more surprised at how hard it can be to get a clear answer. In fact, getting an answer to this question is one of the trickier aspects of client engagement. But this clarity is essential. Because without clarity on the desired outcome, it's nearly impossible to design an effective program, or to be able to tell if the exercise was fruitful or not.

With a clear desired outcome, it is easier to tailor the what, when, where, and how of the learning experience.

This is just as important for you, and it can even be easier to apply. Because you are designing an experience for one, not for many as is the case with larger trainings, your solution can be truly bespoke.

During the predetermination stage, here are the two important questions to ask when you are working by yourself:

- What do I need to know?
- What do I need to be able to do?

With these questions clarified, you have a solid start and you can choose your strategy—book, course, educational provider, format, etc.

For example, if you need to be able to build a wooden bench, then getting a civil engineering degree at a university is probably overkill. Also, it doesn't guarantee that you will be able to perform the task. But reading a book on the subject is probably not enough. An online video course on bench-building is better, but not by much. You are probably best off taking a weekend workshop at a local technical or trades college with a capstone project that involves, well, building a bench. Ease of assessment of learning? Check. Most economical use of resources? Double check.

Of course, there are extensions of these questions to consider depending on your motivation for learning:

- Can I get (or change) jobs with this skill or knowledge?
- How much more could I earn?

- Would this education enable an upward or simply a sideways move within my organization or career?
- Will these skills improve my relationship with my significant other, or my personal life in any way?

All these are valid questions, but they depend on the two foundational questions—what will I know and what will I be able to do?

Step three: PSP

Now you are ready to engage some educational material, whether it be a video, a book, a course, a coach, or lunch with an expert. But how do you ensure you get the most out of the session?

Let's get into an important technique you will apply prior to engaging the material you are trying to learn. I call it Pre-Study Priming (PSP).

A painter uses a primer to prepare a surface to ensure the paint sticks and he achieves the desired result. PSP is a term I have coined to describe statements that you use to prepare your mind for learning. What you want is a fine and finished skillset, not blotches and patches of uneven amateurish gloss. For painting, you use paint primer. For Economical Learning, you use PSP statements.

To be clear, PSP statements are not affirmations like "I learn information quickly and easily" or "I can do whatever I set my mind to". Even though these have their place and many find them useful, PSP is different in that it is a deliberate process where you use language to set your focus prior to engaging the material you are trying to learn. You can also use it to prime yourself before you practice a skill you are trying to master.

The brain "notices" virtually everything around you. However, to keep your conscious mind sane, it filters out most of it and only calls your attention to the things you have determined are important. It's this determination that makes all the difference. On one day, you might determine that shoes are important. On another, ice-cream. For each day, your brain will be filtering out information and presenting you with observations based on what you have chosen to be important. On one day, you see brogues and high-heels everywhere, and on another day during a fast-food lunch break, you ponder what barbeque-flavoured parfait would taste like.

PSP works with the brain by telling it what to look for in a piece of material or during a practice session.

There are two major scenarios in which you will be engaging in learning: acquiring knowledge and practicing that knowledge or skill. PSP can work in both cases. You're activating your brain to seek specific pieces of information to move you towards your desired outcome. Without PSP, you would find yourself rummaging through piles of relevant and irrelevant information with no way of telling one from the other.

It's like trying to put together a jigsaw puzzle with no reference picture of what it's supposed to look like when it's done. You might eventually achieve it, but it will take you twice as long and you will be twice as exhausted!

We'll go into examples of PSP statements later in the chapter but first, let's see how PSP helps you leverage the power of TVF in learning.

PARETO LEARNING AND PSP

How much of the functionality of the tools we use every day are we actually taking advantage of? Think about our cellphones, our cars, our computers, etc. Even the internet. What we use them for on a day-to-day basis is only a small portion of what they are capable of. Yet we get by just fine most of the time with our own little slice. And individuals using the same tools each use different slices of the tool. An accountant may use spreadsheet software very differently from a data modeller, but each person uses the few functions that are vital to them.

The Law of the Vital Few states that a large portion of the results or outputs in a system is produced by a relatively small proportion of inputs. When it comes to the mastery of a subject or skill, the principle holds true. To borrow from Pareto, we can estimate that, for a given skill, you will depend on the execution of 20% of the components of that skill 80% of the time.

Consider team sports. Watch a game of basketball or football and you'll realize that a lot of time is spent moving the ball or puck around the field and between teammates. Without possession of the ball, the team can't score, and so can't win. That's why the highlights of most games last only a few minutes at the most, compared to the hours the full game actually takes. Most of the activity is rather unspectacular. Yet without those unspectacular 80% activities, there would be no 20% highlights. More importantly, players have to master these skills before they can ever have a shot at being good. It's no good being a good "shooter" if you can't pass or dribble.

Being aware of this imbalance upfront can accelerate your learning if you direct your focus and PSP accordingly to what will give you the best return of usefulness.

Here are some incisive questions to consider that will guide your PSP:

- Of all the skills I can learn in this subject, what 20% of those skills would I use 80% of the time?
- What are the three to five core skills that I would use consistently?

These will sharpen your focus going into your engagement with the material. Once you have the answers to these questions, you can move onto priming yourself with a PSP statement.

Examples of PSP statements

Economical Learning is based on the two core questions of "what will I know?" And "what will I be able to do?" Not surprisingly, PSP is related to these two questions.

Below are some examples of PSP statements related to things you want to know, do, or both:

- *I am looking for the core concept of this new idea* (know)
- *I am looking for a way to use this software to balance my financial data* (do)
- *I am looking for information to help me present a five-minute talk on this new subject to my team* (know and do)

Notice that all these examples begin with "I am looking for". By defining what you are "looking for" you are able to recognize it much faster by triggering the brain to notice it. Feel free to replace "looking for" with "searching for" or "listening for" as you prefer.

Earlier, I gave the example of re-reading books in preparation for a speech. There I explained how I might read for the purpose of getting quotes or statistics or stories. Now, if I was reading for quotes, my PSP statement may be:

I am looking for insightful and concise phrases that skillfully articulate a useful or important idea.

Guess what happens when I start to read? I find great quotes on almost every other page.

But what if I had been looking for statistics? Or stories? Well, the interesting thing is, depending on what type of book I read, I will find myself noticing more of what I set out to find than I otherwise would. And for comprehensive and well-written books, it is amazing how much I read into them and—like the quote at the start of this chapter—perhaps more than the author ever intended. That is the power of clear PSP statements.

The ancient maxim is true—*seek and you shall find.*

PSP for understanding

When it comes to understanding, we focus on decoding. We seek to understand the language of the subject we are studying. Even though this is rarely enough, it is a crucial step. Without understanding the concepts involved in something, we will never truly master it.

You can, for example, by trial and error (and a lot of wasted time, energy, and resources) become very good at cooking.

But if you took the time instead to learn the underlying concepts of cooking—the effects of heat on different kinds of foods, how ingredients mix best, etc.—you would master cooking much faster. You would experiment intelligently and innovate ideas in a more sophisticated way. You might even figure out a way to make your barbeque-flavoured parfait dream a reality.

Knowing is not enough

I know a lot about the piano. I can draw you one, name all the keys and tell you how to construct mellifluous chords and progressions. But I can't play the piano to save my life. Sad, I know, but I'm on a mission to learn. For now, what I have is a head full of knowledge. And that is where the music will have to live, instead of out in the air where it can entertain or inspire someone else.

What's the point? Understanding a concept is one thing, applying it in the form of a skill is another. The reality is that knowledge is not as valuable as skill—without application, it's just not very useful. And it is practice that translates knowledge to skill. But you must practice intelligently and economically. You can use PSP before you practice but there are specific principles and how-tos of practice that will skyrocket your results. Let's look at these next.

CHAPTER 13

Purposeful Practice: The Path to Mastery

I started my journey of learning how to swim in my teens—rather late compared to other people. As a high-school student with little cash to my name who was learning to swim in secret (my parents had a fear of me swimming due to a drowning incident that happened in a popular pool around when I was born), I adopted a DIY approach.

I purchased an old used book on swimming, gave it a cursory read, and jumped in the pool. I would splash, and spin, and get a good workout—but I was not getting any better as a swimmer. My cardiovascular health was improving, my lung capacity was definitely growing, as evidenced by my ability to hold my breath for longer underwater as I kicked and pulled furiously—yes, I was *that guy* in the pool—but I was not getting better as a swimmer.

This continued for many weeks. I would sneak into a hotel pool during the day on weekdays because it was less crowded than community rec centers. Sometimes, with the whole pool to myself and no one other than the lifeguard around, I would "practice" my swimming with little to no improvement. The lifeguard would look on quietly.

As time went on, he and I started chatting, perhaps because we were the only ones there. We talked about everyday things and over time built up a good rapport. His name was Ben and he had become a swimmer as a result of being born and raised in a riverine area. That explained his effortless swimming style. Unlike me, he barely made any splashes when he swam and never seemed out of breath no matter how long or fast he went. There was a fluency and effortlessness about his technique that I could only watch in wonder, not even dream of replicating.

One day, I arrived as usual and after working hard but fruitlessly to execute a smooth freestyle stroke, I emerged from the water out of breath and out of patience. Ben called out to me from under his umbrella, "Anthony!" I looked over. Then he made a strange motion with his right arm—a weird, jerky one-armed chicken dance but without the leg motions.

"You look ridiculous," I called back laughing across the pool.

"Raise your elbows! Not your hands!" He replied. "It will help you balance better and reduce the strain on your shoulder."

"Oh! Ok. Thanks!" I replied.

After catching my breath, I tried what he said and even though I didn't quite nail it, I noticed it made a big difference. For the rest of that day, I focused on my elbows, with Ben adding little tips.

"Rotate your body a bit more," he would say, "Relax your wrists."

By the end of the session, I felt like I was swimming better. Unbeknownst to me, I had just had my first brush with a core tenet of practice for expert performance—Purposeful Practice.

PURPOSEFUL PRACTICE, NOT JUST PRACTICE MAKES PERFECT

One of the takeaways from chapter 5 on the TVF Matrix is the call to master the activities in your TVF Sweet Spot. In the pursuit of this mastery, like with most things, there are many more wrong ways to do it than right. In general, if you took a random approach to any endeavour, the odds are largely in favour of you doing it incorrectly.

This is an important driver for people who seek coaching, whether it's for tennis, boxing, personal productivity or public speaking. They don't want to waste time searching for the right way. Because time is valuable, they would rather engage a coach who can save them time, effort, and resources by directing them to the right approaches and techniques to execute correctly and effectively.

That is why I am grateful for the work of experts like Anders Ericsson who have spent decades studying how world-class performers attain their mastery. In his excellent book *Peak: How to Master Almost Anything*, Ericsson introduces a method of practice that is at the heart of developing a skill—Purposeful Practice.

Purposeful Practice is, as the name implies, practicing with purpose. I will briefly outline the markers Ericsson provides that distinguish Purposeful Practice from that type of ad hoc practice so many of us, like me with my swimming, engage in.

Since discovering its effectiveness all those years ago in the pool under the auspices of Ben the lifeguard, it has been invaluable in helping myself and my clients develop skills faster and more effectively. And even if you are not a coach, you might find yourself having to teach a skill at some point in your life—to your kids, a mentee or at work, perhaps.

The principles are central to mastering skills related to *your* Vital Few and attaining your learning goals. This brings us to the first feature of Purposeful Practice.

1. Purposeful Practice has well defined and specific goals

Purposeful Practice involves breaking down a skill into smaller, specific and manageable components, and then systematically setting out to improve our abilities in these areas.

Depending on the skill you are aiming to improve, in yourself or someone else, take some time to think about the components of the skill, and then set goals to improve each aspect. As we have seen from Chapter 12, there are usually a Vital Few that make a big difference, so you may start with them. As you proceed, your goals can focus more and more on finer and finer points.

For me, I was thinking about swimming as one whole skill. However, good swim coaches know that it can be extremely difficult to get a beginner swimmer to practice all the different aspects that go into a smooth and efficient stroke—kicking, body rotation, head, arm and shoulder positioning, breathing, etc.—effectively and in concert. This is why coaches have drills designed to target specific aspects of the swimmer's movements. They allow the swimmer to focus on executing these aspects separately, and then later in concert with other discrete skills. This was what I accidentally started to do with Ben's guidance that day at the pool.

Today, my clients typically have a "big picture" of what they want to achieve—become good speakers or become more effective and productive, for example. But these large goals need to be broken down into smaller, specific components that we can isolate and drill. Without this process of isolation, improvement is slow, and difficult to track.

It's not easy to define what a "good speaker" is or what being "effective" means. But we *can* tell if your gestures are congruent with your words in a section of a speech. And we can determine how many hours are spent a week in the wrong quadrant of your TVF Matrix. Perhaps more importantly, we can actually do something to improve. This applies to you too in whatever skill you are developing—set clearly defined goals for when you practice.

2. Purposeful Practice is focused

There is that f-word again. It seems there is no getting away from focus. It's difficult, if not impossible, to be purposeful without focus. Once you have broken down whatever skill you want to develop into smaller pieces, you must get to work on executing and improving that specific piece.

Focus is the critical facilitator, and distraction the ultimate enemy.

For you, that means giving your *full* attention to the specific aspect of your skill for set bursts of time with the goal of executing that aspect flawlessly.

For me, it meant that I focused *only* on a specific aspect of my stroke at a time giving my full concentration to executing that aspect alone.

Doing this has an impact on the brain. Your brain's neural pathways actually start to morph to make the patterns of electrical signals associated with the action quicker and easier—the more frequently you perform a task with concentration, the easier it becomes. With enough concentrated repetition, the act fades into the background and you appear to do it without thinking about it, which is where you want to be.

I once devised an exercise along these lines for a client who was a brilliant software engineer. Let's call him Dan.

Dan's work had been entered into a conference and stood the chance of winning a prize. His work was good enough to win, but he still had to make a presentation and describe the work to the audience—a task Dan dreaded because he didn't have any experience or skill in public speaking.

Here was a case where Dan's vital few skills in the technical aspects of his work had brought him to a point where his weakest link threatened to do damage. His company engaged me to help him as the paper he was presenting was company-sponsored, and winning the prize would not only be great for Dan but would help the company as well. Our time was limited as the company had informed me of the situation rather late so it became clear we needed to focus on only a few areas that would make the most impact.

After an initial session, I noticed that even though his content was high-quality, his delivery needed work. Specifically, how he structured his points and how he employed (or didn't) non-verbal communication cues. From experience, I knew these would be our lynchpins, especially since the core content was set.

We set to work with Dan focused on converting his content structure from a linear format following the outline of a typical research paper—introduction, materials and methods, results, and discussion—to a narrative structure. Beginning with the question the research asked, we crafted a quest complete with obstacles, plot twists, and cliff-hangers. The *focused practice* was for Dan to present a paragraph of spoken word for each piece of the narrative outline.

An important note here: For this focus to work, we didn't concern ourselves with verbiage, or how to click the slide remote, or even how loud to speak—all valid points of performance in their own right. We focused singly on getting the order of points right to create a compelling narrative. Diluting your focused practice is a sure-fire way to sabotage it. It may feel good for the ego to "practice" many different aspects at the same time. But that is the exact opposite of focus. Resisting this temptation is sometimes harder than the task itself, but it is essential to success.

Once we had that piece down, we moved on to isolating a few key sections of the new outline that would benefit from deliberate non-verbal cues. I then instructed Dan to perform these sections *in complete silence* with focus on the chosen non-verbal actions. He felt funny, to be sure, and we had a few good laughs with jokes about playing high-stakes charades. But the initial awkwardness passed and his gestures and non-verbal expressions became smooth and fluent.

Again, eliminating extraneous cognitive demands, in this case, those related to the recall of words, helped Dan to focus on the non-verbal aspects of his presentation, and to master them. In about an hour of this Purposeful Practice, Dan had completely transformed his presentation and went on to win the award at the conference.

No doubt his victory was mostly on the strength of his research work. But as he told me later, his presentation was very well-received, and he believes that had a lot to do with his mastery of the skills we focused on when we worked together.

The takeaway here is this: When working on developing (or teaching) a complex skill, focus the practice on a specific aspect of that skill to the exclusion of everything else. Practice that aspect in isolation. You can split practice sessions into segments covering different aspects, but during Purposeful Practice, apply what I call OTAT—One Thing at A Time. And for skills that seem more spread out over time (i.e., not really lending themselves to traditional drilling like lap swims or speech rehearsals), this focus continues to apply.

Say you are aiming to increase your productivity. You might spend a set period (a week or even a day) focusing *only* on a predetermined aspect such as checking email at set times of the day to help you focus on high-value work. During this period, you may not bother with other aspects such as regular sleep and wake times, or avoiding sugary snacks, important as they may be. These will get their turn in good time. Instead, you harness your powers to conquer the tyranny of email, and only that. Over many periods of focusing on only one aspect in turn, you will find your effectiveness improve as a whole, greater than the sum of its parts.

If this sounds like I have snuck in a habit-forming hack here, all I can say is, you caught me!

3. Purposeful Practice requires (informed) feedback

Performance is what we put in. Feedback is what we get out, to help improve what we put in. And it is as important, if not more so than the effort we put in, because it helps us get more out of our effort the next time round.

Performance is *what* we are doing, feedback tells us *how* we are doing.

The old saying goes, practice makes perfect. A better expression is perfect practice makes perfect. But without feedback, it's hard to attain perfect practice.

Perfect practice demands evaluating performance against a standard or expectation. The problem is it can get very difficult to perform this evaluation ourselves because we either don't know what the standard is, or we are simply not in a position to objectively judge ourselves against it. There are so many aspects of ourselves that have been parts of us for so long that they have become transparent to our conscious attention. Let me illustrate with an example from my own life.

For my whole life, I had no idea that I had an awkward manner of getting into bed until my wife pointed it out to me some five years into our marriage. Apparently, while most people sit and then lay down horizontally, I lead with my palms and the crown of my head before transferring my lower half and then uncurling my neck and extending the rest of myself to my final resting position. When I asked why she had taken half a decade to tell me, she said it was hilariously entertaining watching me over the years, and she had been worried that if she said something, I might become self-conscious and stop. Still, I appreciated her feedback and have caught myself on occasion starting the comical cascade—sometimes leading to a clumsy and even more amusing attempt to correct on the fly. I suspect she has not regretted her decision to share her feedback.

Now, you probably get into bed like a normal person. But there are aspects of yourself to which you are likely oblivious, and this extends to the performance of skills. This is where having set standards and a means of receiving feedback on how you are doing becomes invaluable.

The good news is that while you almost always need the help of an expert to establish these standards, once set, you can work towards them on your own, and derive the feedback. Given, of course, that you have the tools to do so.

For example, your swim coach may help you determine how many strokes per 25 metres are ideal for your lap. They may also tell you the techniques for performing efficient strokes, as well as point out where you are struggling. With these standards, you can hit the pool with an action camera set up, swim your laps, and self-evaluate against these objective standards. Then you can make adjustments—lengthen your stretch, glide longer, etc.—to get the strokes per 25m to the right number.

What you are trying to do is close the gap between your present level of performance and your desired level. Feedback helps fill these gaps by giving you insight into what you need to do better or differently. It also helps with motivation as that gap between your current and desired level of performance closes. Like Ericsson says:

> Without feedback—either from yourself or from outside observers—you cannot figure out what you need to improve on or how close you are to achieving your goals.

In skill acquisition, having formed the specific goals for your Purposeful Practice, and then applied focus to your practice sessions, it is feedback that informs the tweaks and adjustments that lead to improvement. Even with the first two steps in place, neglecting the critical role of feedback exposes you to the risk of practicing and reinforcing the *wrong* approach to the skill you are trying to develop. This makes it more difficult to improve later as the wrong patterns have become that much more established, possibly even hardened into habits.

Take it from a person who still occasionally hears the muffled chuckles of his spouse as he settles in to sleep at night.

4. Purposeful Practice requires you to step outside your comfort zone

The comfort zone is the realm of competence where we can perform with little or no sense of strain or exertion of physical or mental energy. A good example is driving in familiar areas.

After a few months of learning how to drive and then a few years of driving around a particular city or area, most people are comfortable enough to drive without having to think about it. They commit a minimal level of attention to the mechanics of driving and have more than enough left over to listen to music, an audio-book, carry on a conversation, or even ponder dinner choices as they make their way around a complex network of roads—all this while simultaneously executing a complex motor skill.

Compare these casual drivers to a championship race car driver who spends hours practicing and perfecting his technique of steering, acceleration, and other aspects of driving that we take for granted. For this person, when they practice driving purposefully, they focus with maximum attention. Audiobooks and dinner will just have to wait.

The difference between that driver and the rest of us is that they are *striving* and we have *settled*.

It's this settling that kills improvement, and it is why stepping out of your comfort zone is so critical. More of the same gets you more of the same. In fact, it's unlikely you would have set out to develop a skill in the first place if you didn't feel *un*comfortable with your current level or absence of skill.

The problem is that after a while, we get "good enough" and lose our motivation. This is not entirely bad. Again, sometimes good enough is good enough. But a good enough mindset will frustrate your attempts at Purposeful Practice. Ironically, it appears to be a law of nature that once improvements, even minor improvements, are ignored, deterioration becomes inevitable. In other words, to maintain a level of skill and relevance that is good enough demands that we continue to improve.

We must continually push ourselves, even in little ways, to best our last performance. At an elite level, these minor improvements can make all the difference. For example, over an entire century, the difference in the world record for the 100m race has been just one second. The first record of 10.6 seconds was set by the American, Donald Lippincott in 1912 at the Summer Olympics in Stockholm Sweden. The record set by Jamaican, Usain Bolts in 2009 was 9.58 seconds—just one second faster than the record set almost a century earlier[8]. Between Lippincott and Bolt, there have been thousands of athletes over the years running the 100m race at various levels of competition. But in the final analysis, we realize that it took mankind over 100 years to run 100m one second faster. This might give us an idea of how powerful and difficult seemingly minor improvements can be. And it may also encourage us in light of what we might consider "little" improvements.

It is these little improvements that can keep us going when we find ourselves settling into a comfort zone that stifles our motivation. It's also these little improvements that differentiate mastery from competence.

Purposeful Practice in a nutshell

- To get better at something, we must break down the skill into its components and set specific goals. It helps if these goals are selected with a TVF approach at the outset to maximize the impact, especially where time is short.
- These goals should be set against standards that reflect insight and expertise in the skill.

---

[8] Even though 0.02 seconds is a big deal in the world of elite athleticism, to make the comparison fair, I have approximated to one second here because back in 1912, times were recorded to only one decimal place.

- Next, there needs to be focused practice for each component of the skill.
- This practice must be performed with high-quality feedback supplied which, in turn, informs more focused practice.
- As improvements occur, motivation is needed to not only improve, but even to maintain performance and overcome the dark allure of the comfort zone.

To summarize Ericsson in his own words on Purposeful Practice:

> So here we have Purposeful Practice in a nutshell: Get outside your comfort zone but do it in a focused way, with clear goals, a plan for reaching those goals, and a way to monitor your progress. Oh, and figure out a way to maintain your motivation.

TVF learning and Purposeful Practice, though demanding and requiring deep focus and dedication, are also immensely rewarding. They will help you attain your desired skill level faster. By finding your gaps, defining your Vital Few target abilities, and priming your brain, you will prepare yourself for fruitful study and the application of the proven techniques of Purposeful Practice.

Attempting to get better at your Vital Few skills through shortcuts and quick fixes will not produce lasting results—better to do the work needed so that you get the benefits desired.

Sometimes the longest way round, is the shortest way home.
CS Lewis

BOOK III

TVF RELATIONSHIPS

There is no garment as beautiful as being surrounded by supportive people.

Yoruba saying

No one ever achieved anything great or even good without help. It is physically impossible to do. People need other people to be happy, productive, and fulfilled. These other people will fill different needs and roles in our lives, as we will in theirs. We need people. Period. But not all people matter equally.

You will discover as you read on that TVF exerts itself just as firmly in the realm of our relationships with others as it does in our relationship with ourselves in terms of our practices and activities. Therefore, it is worth considering if and how we are investing in relationships if we are to build balanced and prosperous lives.

CHAPTER 14

Relationship Matters

Most people around you don't matter, but the few that matter, matter a lot.

Now I realize how harsh that sounds. It probably would rank high on the scale of the top ten soundbites to make you sound like a complete jerk. It's definitely not a proclamation to make from the rooftop of your house, otherwise you can forget about being invited to any neighbourhood barbeques.

But let me explain by telling you the story of Haruna.

Haruna is a 43-year-old farmer who lives in the North-Eastern region of Nigeria in a small village. Haruna has three wives—perfectly normal and legal in that part of the world—and 12 children. He is a hard worker, a dedicated family man, and a gentle soul. He is deeply religious, does his best to deal fairly with others and live at peace. And even though he and his entire family of 16 live on less than $5 a day, he lives honestly and tries to instill the same values in his children.

Here's the thing: for most of you reading this book, Haruna does not matter. Until you read this story, you didn't know he existed. You may have known that "people like him" exist, but you didn't know Haruna. And you probably haven't spent any appreciable part of your day thinking about him or others like him. Though he lives, moves, breathes, and on a fundamental level, may even share a lot your values, he simply did not matter. But that's ok. Because to Haruna, you probably don't matter either.

I share the story of Haruna to provide context of what "mattering" means when it comes to relationships. Even people who were, at some point, an incredibly important part of our lives may now be so far in the background as to be virtually forgotten. We certainly do not think about them as often as we used to. And some of the most important people in our lives today—people we live and may even die for—were, at one time, complete strangers. Hard to imagine, isn't it? Yet they have maintained their intrinsic value as human beings, as you have. But their impact, relevance, and influence on your own life, just like yours on theirs, has not been constant.

The discussion here is not of the inherent value of human beings. We all have profound God-given and inalienable intrinsic value. In this sense, *all* people matter a *lot*—we are all priceless and invaluable. I personally believe we all carry divinity within us. Regardless of race, socio-economic status, physical or mental ability, we are all valuable and precious beings.

But what the statement "most people don't matter" means in the TVF sense is that while *all* people are intrinsically valuable, they can't all be practically valuable to every other human being equally. That is, in terms of who matters to you personally—to your wellbeing, your happiness, your success—the number shrinks dramatically from *all* to *a Vital Few*. In this sense, only a *few* people matter, but they matter a lot.

The call is not to discount the value of others, but to get very deliberate about how we manage our relationships based on our values and goals so that we don't make the error of spending our energy on the wrong people at the expense of the vital few that really matter; to realize that we cannot be all things to all people and no person can be all things to us. Because as much as we might not like to admit it, there is really only so much we can handle effectively when it comes to our relationships. Coming to terms with this is the first and vital shift that needs to happen if we want to be successful in making the most of these relationships.

COMEDY OF INSIGHTS

In the hit comedy show of the 90s, *Seinfeld*, the main character, Jerry Seinfeld, had a funny but insightful interaction. Fans of the Seinfeld show know that it revolves around the core character and a handful of supporting characters, most of whom are acquainted with each other, but who all share an acquaintance with Seinfeld himself.

There was George, Jerry's closest friend; Elaine, ex-girlfriend turned best-buddy; the eccentric neighbour Kramer; and the archnemesis, postal worker, Newman. Then, there were Seinfeld's parents who would make occasional appearances, as would members of the core group's family from time-to-time. But other than Jerry's transient dalliances, the cast stayed pretty stable, and part of the genius of the show was the ability to make rather mundane interactions between this group so hysterical.

In one episode—*The Pool Guy*—Seinfeld bumped into an acquaintance, Ramon, from his health club. Ramon then attempts to befriend Seinfeld. After many thwarted advances, the tension mounts until finally, in his signature smug style, Seinfeld candidly informs Ramon that he has enough friends in his life and really cannot handle any more. Perhaps symbolically, Seinfeld delivers the lines across closing subway train doors after stepping off the train he and Ramon had been riding in.

I know you are not writhing with side-splitting laughter when you read it like this, but comedy is 50% delivery. I can tell you the entire thing was quite funny.

But beyond giggles, the episode aptly showcases the main idea behind our exploration of the Vital Few relationships—we all have a limited capacity when it comes to how many relationships we can truly nurture.

EMOTIONAL BANDWIDTH

Bandwidth is a term that has become commonplace thanks to the rise of the internet. The technical details get complicated but, as I have had it patiently explained to me, bandwidth is simply a measure of how much information a network can handle at a time.

This information is referred to, rather unimaginatively but thankfully simply, as "bits" or "bytes". 1000 bytes is 1kB; 1,000,000 is 1MB; 1,000,000,000 is 1GB; and 1,000,000,000,000 is 1TB. There are only so many bits a bandwidth can convey at a time, and this is the source of the curious numbers that internet companies use to market their "connection speeds". A 1gb/s connection, for example, can relay one million bits of information in one second.

That is why you can download multiple text documents with little issue, because text documents tend to have small file sizes. But if you're downloading a large ultra-HD video in one window of your browser, you may encounter difficulty if you simultaneously attempt to stream another video in a second window. It's not the speed per se that's at play—it's your bandwidth that is being taxed. The first heavy download is using up a lot of your bandwidth and not leaving you enough for the second—you simply don't have enough capacity to handle both.

But it's not only internet connections that have limited bandwidths. Our social connections do too, including the ones exclusively on social media that also rely on bits/second connections.

We have limited *emotional* bandwidth—we can only handle so many downloads from our emotional resources at a time. And the more capacity each connection takes up in our bandwidth, the less we have left for other connections.

If you have a family or a close friend, you know this all too well. They can be very rewarding and satisfying, but also emotionally taxing at times. And anyone who has had to care for an ailing loved one knows how much it drains one emotionally to the point of affecting other relationships.

———————————

Our emotional wellbeing is key to our overall wellbeing. So much so that, for many of us, it is incredibly difficult to be productive—cognitively or otherwise—if we are in bad emotional shape. Even though there is an immense amount of personal responsibility to be taken for our emotional state, it is impractical and just flat out wrong to think that our relationships with other people do not play a role in how we feel.

Consequently, our quality of life is directly affected by the quality of our relationships. In fact, relationships with others consistently ranks very high as a marker for happiness and wellbeing. More so than even material possessions.

YOUR CORE

Let's do an exercise. Make a list of the people in your life starting with the most important to the (ahem) least. For example, near the top of the list might be your spouse, your children, your siblings, and parents. And nearer the bottom might be your grocery store checkout clerk. Self-checkout doesn't count.

Your list is unique to you of course, these are just guidelines. Take a moment to do that now.

Next, look at the top five names on that list and look at your calendar for the last month. How much of your time did you spend with them? And how meaningful was the time? That is, think about the quantity and the quality of time you spent with them. How do the results make you feel? I remember doing this a few years back and being fairly disappointed.

Most people simply are not investing time in the relationships that matter to them the most, all the while being oblivious to the fact. Sadly, the people who are the closest to us are the ones we take for granted the most. We believe they have been and will always be there. But that's not true—neglected relationships are prone to deteriorate. We understand that everything, from our relationships to our cars, needs conscious maintenance. Yet some of us schedule our oil changes religiously, but don't make time to service our relationships. Instead, we neglect them.

What constitutes neglect for one kind of relationship may be more than enough to maintain another kind of relationship. You may want to spend more time with your growing child than with your friend, Grace. Going two weeks without having a meal with your child might be unacceptable to you, but it's probably fine if you and Grace only chow down together every few weeks or so. The question is, are you happy with how much time you are investing in the relationships you value?

It may seem obvious to suggest that we should invest the most in the people closest to us and the people we value the most. But as obvious as it may seem, isn't it the norm to put these people last? Especially when we are under pressure from outside forces? How often do parents cancel attending a child's sporting event or spelling bee to go on a business trip instead? And how often do we cancel date night with our significant other because we have to work late?

I'm not saying that doing these things is right or wrong, but I am asking you to reflect on where the most important people in your life stand—not in your intangible ideal, but in your day-to-day schedule. Do you make time for the people you say matter the most? If not, why not? And what will you do right now to start turning that pernicious tide?

It might seem odd to ask you to book time in your calendar to spend with your loved ones, maybe even transactional and uncool. But as life gets busier and busier, we find that what is not scheduled is not done. If you are already a Rockstar in this aspect, congratulations. But if you find yourself struggling or juggling, then try this out: schedule quality time with your loved ones in your diary or calendar, and honour it. You will be surprised how much of a positive impact it can make not only in their lives, but yours as well.

As you practice the principles of TVF, you will create more space in your life, but in the meantime, I encourage you to start to use some of the space you have now to strengthen your core relationships. This is one investment you can be confident you will not regret.

CAREER RELATIONSHIPS: A CHAT WITH A CAREER CONSULTANT

Ann Nakaska is a career consultant who specializes in career decision-making and career planning. Her company, Constructive Career and Life Designs, helps her clients navigate the different aspects of changing jobs or careers. Ann has been helping clients become career explorers, decision-makers, and strategists for over 15 years.

I called Ann to discuss why people (her clients) transitioned jobs and careers. Specifically, I wanted to know how much of a role workplace relationships played in people's decisions to exit their jobs.

"It is not just my clients who leave jobs because of relationships," Ann started. "I myself started down this career path in large part due to relationships. As I got into this world, I found that the people I was interacting with and the passion and messages of the thought-leaders and influencers made me feel like I had found my tribe. And I had."

She went on, "Not only was this the work I knew I wanted to do, but I also knew these were the kind of people I could work with. Over the years, I have built relationships with many of the industry's influencers and engaged with industry associations."

Ann believes deeply in the importance of working first on the relationship that matters the most—the one workers have with themselves. One important point that came out of my chat with Ann was that regardless of whom you are interacting with, it is critical to understand that you cannot really manage any relationship. What you *can* do is manage *yourself* in those relationships. It is important to pull the locus of control towards yourself. Self-regulation, thoughtfulness, conscientiousness, attentiveness, empathy, adaptability, kindness are all qualities that reside within us. And when they are developed, they can bring out the best in others as well.

Still though, personalities matter in choosing a field. Ann told me, "Human resource professionals are big on personality tests and matching people to professions based on these tests. Career professionals have been using these tests long before they became popular. There are many types of tests with different classifications, and one thing you notice over and over again from the results is that certain professions attract certain personality types, regardless of the test you use."

Ann shared the story of one of her relatives who had a personality type that was in the minority in the general population. Not surprisingly, he was not very well-suited to a lot of mainstream careers. But when this individual joined a seminary, he discovered that he was in a group where the *majority* shared his personality trait. Suddenly, he felt at home and was doing what not only brought him a deep sense of joy and fulfilment, but also put him in contact with others of a like-mind—an important factor for enjoying one's work and life.

But it's not always as simple as that. Ann said sometimes we have a general idea of what would be a good fit for us but there can be nuances that affect how we will experience the work and the people we will encounter.

"Take police officers and lawyers, for example," Ann explained. "Both professions are connected to the law but in different ways and so attract different types of people. Police officers tend to be more hands-on, and lawyers more conceptual in their approach."

Ann told me about an important aspect of her process with clients that highlights this subtlety. Over her 15 years of helping clients take a more proactive approach to their careers, she has developed four key questions that she uses to open the exploration with a client considering a job or career change:

- Do you like the industry you work in?
- Do you like the company you work for?
- Do you like the job you do?
- Do you like the people, including your boss, that you work with?

"So you think relationships are *that* important?" I asked Ann.

"I think all four are interrelated," Ann replied. "It's important for people to know who they are as a clue to knowing what kind of work will be suitable to them, not only from the perspective of skills but relationships as well. It's challenging when the divide is too wide between one's own personality and those matched to success in an industry, company, or job. That just increases the chances that you won't be able to contribute and collaborate effectively with others."

"How important are relationships in these terms?" I asked. "Do people ever come to you seeking job or career changes just on the basis of relationships?"

"Relationships matter a lot. Not only is it important from a peer perspective, but also especially with bosses."

Ann shared the story of a client of hers we'll call Sue. Sue had worked in the healthcare industry in Alberta for over three decades and was five years away from retirement. She had been a successful nurse and enjoyed working with fellow nurses until she got a new boss who made her miserable. As someone who had worked that long, Sue had seen many bosses and had been able to work well with them. But this one was insufferable. Sue was having such a bad time of it, that she was considering quitting.

After analyzing Ann's four questions, Sue realized she was throwing away a career she loved, in a hospital she loved, an industry she loved and co-workers she loved, because of one relationship. She chose instead to develop adaptive strategies and influence skills to help her cope and "manage up", as they say.

"She was only a few years from retirement anyway. It made no sense from a purely practical standpoint to quit. Besides, as my relationship with Sue as a client deepened, it became clear she really did love her industry, company, and the people she was working with—all but this one person. She also really enjoyed her work."

"And she was going to pack it in so close to retirement?" I asked.

"It's hard to overestimate how much of an impact a toxic relationship can have on our work, especially when the other party is a person in authority. That's why, where possible, we must not only nurture positive relationships with our peers, but also with those above us. Even better than bosses are role models and mentors. Those are not always the same as the people we report to. They represent more of an ideal, someone we look up to. Building relationships with those people can be immensely rewarding in a variety of ways."

"And what about people who like their bosses and colleagues? What advice do you give them when they come to you seeking a career change?"

"After all these years, I have not had a single client that matches that bill. People who truly like the people they work with are not likely to be trying to make a career change, so I guess I wouldn't be seeing them."

I can summarize my conversation with Ann in two key points:

- In making your career choice, don't leave out the vital role of your personality and how it will mesh (or not) with the kind of work and the kind of people in the work. Go *in* before you go *out*.
- In whatever career you find yourself, relationships are critical—nurture horizontally and vertically. Nurture relationships with peers as well as leaders and mentors. Go *up* and *side to side*.

Though Ann didn't mention it, her observations and insights are in line with one of the most influential ideas in the motivational theory of work: Self Determination Theory (SDT).

According to the developers of the theory, Edward L. Deci and Richard Ryan, motivation can come from both intrinsic (internal) and extrinsic (external) factors. On the intrinsic side, there are three important factors that affect a person's level of motivation in their work:

1. **Autonomy:** How much control a person has over when, where, and how they do their work.
2. **Competence:** How confident a person feels in regards to performing the work.
3. **Relatedness:** The need to have close, meaningful relationships with others.

The theory holds that when these three areas are in good shape, a person is more likely to feel motivated and fulfilled at work. And while two out of the three (autonomy and competence) address the work itself, the third one is clearly all about relationships.

Relationship-directed careers

The Gallup Corporation, founded in the United States in 1958, is a company that is known the world over for its public opinion and workplace polls. Initially focussed on public opinion polls to predict the outcome of US elections, since the late 80s, Gallup has moved in the direction of serving businesses. They now provide business analytics services, management consulting, and workplace strengths assessments. Their website boasts having over 35 million respondents to one of their most popular workplace polling offerings—their employee engagement survey.

I took one of these surveys in an old job. All the questions seemed plausible and commonsensical; when was the last time you were acknowledged by a leader? How clearly do you understand your role? All pretty run-of-the-mill for an employee engagement survey. But then there was one question that surprised me, at least initially, but a little thought revealed it as a no-brainer. The question was: Do you have a best friend at work?

This seemingly simple question offers some illumination in our exploration of the place of relationships in your Vital Few. As I read it on that survey, I immediately thought about Kelly.

Kelly and I were true work buddies. We had lunches together semi-regularly as well as frequent coffee breaks and chats where we talked about everything from office matters to our families to our favourite shows streaming on Netflix. As I thought about the question from the survey and my relationship with Kelly, I could see why an employee engagement survey, especially one as highly-rated as Gallup, would pick up on this nuance of workplace engagement and employee satisfaction.

From the employer's perspective, when workers have meaningful relationships at work, they tend to work better and are less likely to leave the job. In this light, having a meaningful relationship as an indicator of engagement and wellbeing makes perfect sense.

For the individual, aside from having someone close at hand to book lunch and coffee breaks with, celebrate successes with, and occasionally complain to and let off some work steam with, there is a simple math factor when it comes to time spent.

We spend a large portion of our days at work, more than enough to impact the rest. Therefore, for the very practical reason that we spend a long time at work, we might as well be happy there. A full-time job in North America requires around 40 hours a week. On a five-day workweek, that comes to eight hours a day. This is where the playful label for a steady job—a 9 to 5—comes from. Of course, many people work flexible shifts of varying hours, some work part-time meaning fewer hours, and others work much longer hours than this. Still, most people spend around eight hours a day at work. And unless they run a family business, it's unlikely they are spending this time with family. We also spend around another eight hours sleeping. The fact that we spend around half of our waking hours at our jobs or at least engaged in some activity related to earning a living for a large portion of the week should indicate to us how important these work relationships are.

How likely you are to form meaningful relationships at work is hardly a precise science. Most people will tell you they don't want to work with difficult colleagues or bosses. But once we consider that different careers tend to attract people of a certain temperament, we see how we might be more likely to be dealing with our own version of "difficult people" if we choose a career that attracts that type. We thereby inadvertently put ourselves in a position to experience a lot of stress.

This consideration is important enough to direct our careers. Perhaps you've heard of people who have left not just jobs but careers in certain fields because they didn't like the "type" of people who work in those jobs or fields. Part of the frustration may come from the actual work; a person might lack the technical skills to succeed or it might be because of the time demands of certain careers. But other times, people simply quit because they can't stand the people in those fields.

Even working the same job in different industries, as we can glean from Ann's four questions, can yield different experiences, money and prestige aside. I personally know people who have quit high-paying jobs and even switched careers because they were put off by the exaltation of profit above all else—even ethics—by the people they worked with and reported to in that line of work.

Yet, the "type of people who work in this field" is not a common consideration when most people consider their careers, at least not in the earlier stages. But who you work with might be just as important as where you work and what you do.

For one, it affects your odds of having good work relationships and work friends, and this has a big impact on your sense of wellbeing and even relevance at work. It's not uncommon for people to put up with lower pay and difficult work tasks because they have built meaningful relationships with leaders and colleagues. The human resources mantra of "people don't quit jobs, they quit managers" may not be all-encompassing, but it definitely holds true to a large extent.

Perhaps you are thinking to yourself, "But I'm not an employee, I'm an entrepreneur." This still matters.

I know that as my business grew, I had to give careful thought to the type of client I wanted to attract to my coaching business as well as the ideal audience I wanted to speak to. I realized I was better off having fewer clients (the Vital Few) whom I could work closely and effectively with to produce results, than trying to serve many who might be a bad fit. And when it comes to audiences, the more I know about them, the more successful I can be at speaking with them.

As an entrepreneur, you will have to make the same type of decisions. Who you will serve with your product or service will determine the entire chain of human contact you will have. Outsourcing is a common response to this. But even if you outsource everything, you will still have service vendors to deal with. And even if your business grows to the point where you can hire people to deal with those vendors, you might have to deal with business stakeholders—board members, for example—as well as those people you hired.

In the course of doing your work, whether it be a job or a business, there is simply no getting away from relationships. Depending on your temperament, you might see this as a blessing or a necessary evil. I think it's a blessing. Relationships can be immensely rewarding in various ways and add a depth and meaning to life and work that is hard to fill any other way. But that's just me.

In the end, we must decide what type of people we want to work with and what kind of work relationships we want. These decisions have a major impact on the kind of work we pursue and how successful we are at it. We need people and relationships of varying degrees of closeness in our careers, from close-working clients and colleagues to perhaps more removed customers or vendors to board members.

Working with the right kind of people—the kind you can build good relationships with fairly easily—will be beneficial for growing a strong network that can expand your horizons and lead to large leaps forward in your career or business. This is what it means to look at our work through the lens of relationships.

But we can also make relationship decisions through the lens of our careers or business. That is, investigating the relationships that are the Vital Few for success in our fields, and then investing wisely in nurturing those relationships appropriately.

Career-directed relationships

As we have seen, the kind of relationships we want to have can be a decisive factor in the kind of work we give ourselves to— our relationship-directed careers. But once we have chosen our path, we need to determine what key relationships will help us succeed—our career-directed relationships. Depending on your goals for your career, some relationships will matter much more than others.

Our current career landscape is experiencing unprecedented tectonic shifts. A few thousand years ago, your career options were limited. In fact, you had only one tripartite option: hunter-gather-warrior. This was about as diverse as the workforce got. As we moved on to establish larger societies with agriculture taking off and artisanship gaining ground, you had more choices: farmer, ironsmith, goldsmith and many other "smiths", baker, labourer, and eventually, banker, inventor, philosopher, professor, etc. These vocations varied in the level of skill they required. But even up to the last few hundred years, career paths were fairly linear with life progressing smoothly from learning years (when you get an education in a certain field), to earning years (when you work a job, usually at the same place for several decades), to conclude quietly in yearning years (when you retire and live off a good pension or retirement savings).

Today, your career is unlikely to follow one linear path. In fact, the odds have shifted in favour of you having not just one career, but many—each with its own path, people, and relationships.

Take some time right now to reflect on where you are in your career or business. Are there important relationships you are neglecting? Are there clients, partners, bosses, or colleagues you could invest in just a little more? It could be as small as an occasional 30-minute coffee chat. These little investments can go a long way in strengthening your network.

One important tip in this regard: **come into every interaction with the mindset of at least *mutual* benefit.** Nothing turns people off more than a sense of being exploited.
Be at least:

- as willing to give as you are to receive,
- as willing to listen as you are to speak, and
- as respectful as possible.

By practising this, over time, you will earn the respect of your network. They will think favourably of you, and that is a good thing.

As you develop your Vital Few relationships, strengthen your core—the relationships with those closest to you. These people matter the most to you so make time and space for them for your good and theirs. Also, be intentional about the role your work relationships play in your life not only as a force of choice, but also as a strategy for sustaining a long and meaningful career. And remember, if you ever had to leave a job, pursue a promotion, or start a business venture, a lot of your opportunities will come from your connections. Sometimes, from your loose connections.

CHAPTER 15

Nurture Loose Connections, a Little

Katt Williams is regarded as one of the most skillful stand-up comedians in the business. Even through his rocky and controversial personal life, it is hard to deny his comedic artistry evidenced by his ability to fill large venues and have the audience in stitches mere minutes into a show. His over-the-top, rakish outfits and masterfully exaggerated physicality combined with clinically crafted lines, rat-tat-tat delivery delights, and his incisive social commentary makes you think and rethink even while you laugh. But behind his seemingly free-form, off-the-cuff conversational comedic style lies a wealth of technique. When you watch him, patterns start to emerge.

One thing is consistent when he opens his show—he gives a shoutout to the city he is performing in. But it is the way he words his shoutouts that is important.

In his Netflix Special, *Great America,* performed and filmed live in Jacksonville, Florida, he begins with a nod to the city, "I have done seven, eight specials. Nothing is messing with Jacksonville at all! Let me say that off the top." Notice that he doesn't say nothing is messing with the *residents* of Jacksonville. But simply nothing is messing with Jacksonville.

For the earlier and mega-successful Pimp Chronicles filmed in Atlanta Georgia, he begins, "It's a pleasure to be out here in Atlanta and just look at you..."

For *American Hustle* filmed in Chicago Illinois, he starts, "What's going on Chicago? What's going down?"

What's more interesting than this odd choice of wording is the audience's reaction. They love it! They cheer, wave, and woot, just at the mention of their city.

Many other successful comedians and even non-comedic acts in music and stage play also employ some version of this in their shows, especially if they are touring acts.

So, what's going on here? Why does acknowledging the city produce such a powerful and rather predictable response?

What's happening is the performer is tapping into what psychologists call "group identity". The performer wants to use the most certain common denominator to unite the audience and engage them. With increasing demographic diversity in big cities, and with so many potential divisions—sex, race, religion, culture, etc.—the sure-fire denominator becomes the city itself. Not everyone in the audience will be from the city or even live there, but it's safe to assume that most will and so will share this group identity. And for those who do, their acknowledgement is an affirmation of that group identity—a response to a kind of call to the tribe from the performer.

However, "group identity" is rather broad, covering everything from the tight identity of members of a strict religious order, to the weaker identity of simply living in the same city. That is why I like to call this weaker brand of group identity "loose connections". Leveraging this loose connection, the performer creates a cohesion and a sense of harmony that is so crucial to performance in general and comedy in particular.

What does this have to do with your Vital Few relationships? Well, here is where there is a twist in the story—I suggest you nurture a larger number of relationships. But not to worry, you will only do so loosely.

LOOSE CONNECTIONS AND HOW
TO START A REVOLUTION

It's impossible to make a real and lasting impact without loose connections. Entrepreneurs know they cannot count only on friends and family to buy their products or services if they plan to be successful. They rely heavily on loose connections, whether that be connections to vendors or customers.

Your inner circle of relationships—your core—is, by definition, not large enough to buy enough of whatever you are selling to earn a good living. Loose connections—those casual acquaintances and friend-of-a-friend kind of relationships—provide the kind of networking and multiplication effect that enables your message, services, product, or brand to reach more people than it could ever otherwise do. It's also through these loose connections that some of the most profound social changes are propagated.

In his book on habits mentioned earlier, Charles Duhigg points to loose connections (what he calls weak ties) as important catalysts of social transformation. He tells the story of Rosa Parks in Montgomery Alabama in the United States, the iconic black woman who took a stand by refusing to give up her seat on the bus to a white person, as was the law of the time for people of colour. Her subsequent arrest sparked outrage in the community and went on to mark an important inflection point for the civil rights movement. Duhigg describes the crucial role that Rosa's loose connections to her church, neighbours, social groups, and clubs played in the chain of events that transpired after her arrest—the chain that ultimately overturned some of the unjust laws subjugating the black community of the south in America. This is not a one-off. Loose connections are a critical part of a process that appears again and again when sociologists and historians have studied social change. It appears that without them, it is difficult for ideas to spread.

You might be trying to change legislation or start a revolution, or you might not. You might just want to get your brand or product "out there" or make strides forward in your professional life. The realization that there is power latent in your loose connections should encourage you to grow and nurture this vital side of your relationships.

The gift of belonging

When my father passed away in 2007, it was one of the most important events in my life. It was at once one of the saddest, most informative, and most revealing experiences I have ever had. I was just finishing my undergraduate studies and got the call while on campus informing me that he had passed away after a long stint at the hospital. So, I wrote my finals and packed up my bag for the trip back home to the family house in Kano, Nigeria.

Being the youngest of five, I was not really involved with the planning or logistics of the burial. So, when the day came, I was surprised to see just how many people showed up to help. In fact, my immediate family—mother and siblings—felt like we were simply *attending* the burial about as much as anyone else was. So many people showed up to help that we all had very little to do as far as the planning and proceedings.

There was no doubt that my father nurtured close and important family and business relationships very deliberately. He also, however, belonged to and contributed in many ways to his church, and was an avid and long-time member of the first Rotary Club to be established in the country, remaining an active member right up till his passing. He also supported charities and other social groups.

In retrospect, we, his family, never felt like these communities were keeping him away from us. If anything, they gave us a lot of options for what Christmas parties to attend, each furnishing its own helping of scrumptious cuisine. There was also lots of entertainment—the best of which were not the organized acts and displays, but rather the unintentional gaffes that provided plenty of recap laughter in the car ride home. That's on top of the Christmas parties we inevitably threw ourselves and had to help clean up after. Come to think of it, dad had a mysterious way of disappearing during the clean-up part.

But back to my point. These associations never really took him away from us in a disruptive way. He would have the occasional meeting in the evenings or on a Saturday morning, but we still got plenty of dad around to have meals and arguments over soccer club superiority with. In other words, while dad maintained a strong core with his family as best he could, he also nurtured loose connections deliberately. So that when he passed away, people showed up.

Members of the church community created a 15-car convoy around the hearse and carried a banner announcing his passing as they drove to the funeral. To give you an idea, the first time I set eyes on the banner was on the morning of the funeral. The entire ceremony unfolded in pretty much the same pattern. At every point in the proceedings, there were people taking care of business. People showed up for him and for us. And most of them I didn't even know. They were loose connections. Seeing all those people—some of them strangers—show up and support and celebrate his life was at once inspiring and instructive to me. It made me think about the power of loose connections and how important they are in living a life that matters. It made me think about all the times over the years when some of these loose connections have led to important breakthroughs in his business, times when he had drawn on them or they had showed up to ease the solution of a problem.

So, I offer this suggestion to you in pursuing the Vital Few way of life—join groups and communities that resonate with you. These could be communities in your neighbourhood or communities based on shared interests or beliefs. Engage your local church if you are a person of faith, join a book club if you enjoy reading, or a camera club if you enjoy photography (or at least, like talking about it). Find clubs and communities with common interests and, importantly, common values you could commit and belong to. Volunteer with charities if that's your inclination.

Belong to something you find interesting and meaningful.

It can prove to be a generous source of personal happiness and fulfilment. Belonging means being consistent and dependable, and for most communities, it also means being supportive and helpful of the other members of the community. This is more than networking, it's belonging.

With belonging though, there are a few caveats to be wary of lest they sabotage your TVF way of life.

1. The creep

The saying goes the reward for good work is more work. And that is true even in non-paying work which is what most of these communities are. As your commitment and contribution are recognized, there will almost certainly be requests for more of each. Beware the creep.

It's a good idea to decide in advance how much time and energy you are willing to commit, and then hold yourself to that. You can adjust as needed, perhaps you even *want* to get more involved if the community proves to be a potential candidate for your TVF Sweet Spot. You have control, but be intentional.

2. The temptation of too many

In keeping with the theme of doing less to do more, be careful not to belong to *too* many clubs or communities. Perhaps you have many interests; instead of draining yourself and falling into the Trivial Many, create a plan staggering each interest over time so that you are not trying to belong to all the potential communities at the same time.

The good news is that even if you have to leave one community to pursue your interest in another, you can continue to nurture connections loosely by staying in touch with individuals from the community you are exiting. Just because you're leaving a group doesn't mean you have to leave every single person in that group. Speaking of leaving…

3. The temptation of being assimilated

Communities have a group identity. Some are not as strong as others; some are downright stifling. If you ever feel like your liberty is being strangled or unreasonable demands are being made beyond how much you are willing to stretch, do not hesitate to leave. To paraphrase Emmet Fox, the only allegiance you owe is to the integrity of your soul.

Even with these caveats, belonging to the right groups remains an important way to build and nurture loose connections, and to extend our reach beyond our immediate circle. But not every loose connection will come about through belonging to a group. Sometimes, the most rewarding experiences from loose connections come back to us as a result of a simple good deed.

The power of kindness: do unto others

It's difficult to quantify the power of an act of kindness. It brings immense joy to both the giver and the recipient. In fact, research shows that even *witnesses* of an act of kindness experience powerful and positive emotions. So giver, receiver and onlooker all benefit from acts of kindness—which is only a recognition of *kin*ship to our fellow humans.

Yet in our busy lives, it's easy to forget kindness. In the pursuit of goals, accomplishments, and prestige, it's easy to fall into the trap of seeing people as, at best, part of the landscape and, at worst, tools to be manipulated for our own ends. The first point of view may lead us to ignore people and to live in our bubble with no regard or thought for those around us unless their existence directly impacts us in some way. The second point of view may lead us down a destructive path of manipulation where we treat only the right people right—the right people being the people we can get something from.

Neither is true nor wise. The better way is to adopt kindness. To realize that people—all people, you, me and everyone else—are kin. We are all trying our best to navigate this complex and often bewildering world with the best tools we have at our disposal. Adopting a posture of kindness can help us lend a helping hand to the people that come our way, from strangers to colleagues and confidants.

Sometimes that gift of kindness comes back to reward us tenfold, as we hear told in countless real-life stories and fables alike. Other times the reward is only the satisfaction of knowing that we helped somebody else along the way.

If you are of a mystic or religious inclination, you may call it Karma or The Golden Rule. If you subscribe to a Darwinian viewpoint, you may call it reciprocity. I call it kindness. And though its benefits may be hard to graph, its positive impact on us and those around us is as clear as the light of day.

ANCIENT WISDOM FOR MODERN TIMES

The Yoruba are a tribe in Western Africa well known for their exacting taste and skill in weaving fabrics. Cloth weaving has been a staple form of artistic expression and economic trade among these people since the 15th century.

One of their signature creations is the iconic aso oke (that translates as the cloth from the hinterland or "high" cloth). It's intricately woven from cotton through a process exclusive to the Yorubas with looms and techniques passed down through families from generation to generation. Most of the process for making aso oke is still completed by hand by specialized craftspeople today.

The Yoruba value presentation and take pride in their craft and dress. In fact, there is a long-standing joke that one of the worst fates to befall a spectator at an event is to be seated behind a Yoruba woman. Why? Well, because her headdress would be so large and flamboyant that the unfortunate soul would see nothing of the show!

But even the Yorubas knew that relationships are a better covering than any fancy clothing. They have a saying that translates loosely as: "There is no garment as beautiful as people. Being surrounded by (supportive) people is like being clothed in honour and glory."

The Yorubas have been saying this for centuries, long before cell phones, social networking, and email. Yet in modern times, this is more important than ever. As life gets faster and more fluid, stable and solid relationships remain invaluable. Not only do these relationships provide a much-needed infusion of positive emotional energy, but they can also be crucial to helping us bounce back from a setback resulting from an unexpected tide of change. They are truly a covering more beautiful than clothing.

Tend to this vital asset—the people in your life.

FINAL WORDS

There are many today who are living decidedly average lives, and many others leading lives of quiet desperation. If mediocrity is pleasing to you, that's a different conversation. But it is those who want more but cannot seem to attain it that I am concerned with here. Those who can feel the tension between their current and ideal selves—those who want to do, be, have, and give more, but find themselves struggling, constantly distracted or frustrated.

Sometimes these frustrations come from the very practical demands of earning a living or maintaining a level of material comfort. Other times, it's a result of social pressures. All of which can cause us to feel like we are constantly catering to the agendas of others and not our own.

Whether your pressures are financial or social, remember that as strange as it may sound, you can always make more money. What you cannot make is more time—you cannot make more life. You can always make new friends in your lifetime, but you cannot make new lifetimes. Your greatest asset is not your car, your house, your stocks, or your degrees. It is *you*. And as we have seen, what and who you give yourself to determines whether you appreciate or depreciate.

I dream of a world where every person is doing their best work. The work that sits squarely in the center of their Vital Few. Doing this, each person gives themselves the best life possible. They give the world the greatest value possible. And we are all better off for it.

We live in an incredibly amazing time. Technologically, we have never been more advanced. Computing power only available to spaceships less than a hundred years ago is now available in our cell phones. And that's just technology. Socially, economically, intellectually, while we are far from perfect, we have made great progress. There are more opportunities open to more people on the planet now than have ever been. The prior physical barriers of time and space have been all but removed. All this opens up immense opportunities for us to exploit. In an earlier chapter, I hinted at how this ease of access can be dangerous because it tempts us to do many things, spread our energies thin, and never really narrow down to our Vital Few. But there is a second side to this coin.

If we can get over the hurdle of distraction by variety, we can take long strides towards the goal of mastery in whatever field we choose.

What makes the difference between mere dabbling and distinction is focus and determination. And that comes when your decision to embark on your quest is educated by a thorough exploration of your Vital Few. Knowing that your efforts are being invested in your Vital Few will motivate you to exert that effort with a calm confidence in an exponential yield of returns—you will know that the deck is stacked in your favour.

If you do find yourself struggling with the notion of living differently, console yourself in knowing that once you hit your stride, this too will become normal for you. It will soon become normal for you to evaluate your options through the lens of the Vital Few. And perhaps more importantly, it will become normal for you to act in line with your Vital Few and by so doing, reap the benefits.

Changes that seem difficult initially as we embark on a journey of growth and improvement very soon become normal. Especially as we begin to enjoy the gains.

Wholesome success—the kind that comes from a balanced life of prosperity, contribution, and serenity—is incredibly addictive, the kind of thing people don't give up easily. We are just as good at adapting to positive changes as we are to negative ones. Maybe even better. After all, we don't use the expression "I could get used to this" for undesirable experiences, but for positive changes.

One thing I do know is that you *can* change if you *want* to change. Some days will be easy, others a bit hard. Trivial pursuits will rear their heads and people will pressure you to cave in. And sometimes you will. That's ok. This is not a call to perfection, but to reflection and guided action. Each time you find yourself missing the mark, recompose and refine your approach.

There will be mistakes. But if you keep pressing, you will keep getting better. As this way of life becomes your new normal, you will reach higher and higher, achieve more, give more, become more. And hopefully, as your success multiplies, it will fuel your motivation to go even deeper in the practice of The Vital Few. And that is a good thing.

ABOUT THE AUTHOR

Anthony Sanni is a consultant, professional speaker, and coach specialized in helping people and organizations harness the power of personal productivity and maximize their presentation skills.

He holds degrees in Industrial Chemistry and engineering. It was this exposure to science and engineering that first got him interested in the study of systems and models for making things more productive. But through his work in those fields, Anthony found himself becoming increasingly interested in another type of system—the human system. Specifically, the question: How can we make *ourselves* more productive so we can have more to give and enjoy?

This, in combination with his love for public speaking, led Anthony to abandon his previous professional life and embark on a new career in which he helps others discover the answers to this question. This book is a culmination of his work in this area.

Anthony is a dynamic and sought-after speaker at conferences and events where he delivers top-rated keynotes, seminars, and workshops.

He lives in Calgary, Alberta with his wife and two daughters.
Keep up to date with his work by visiting:
www.anthonysanni.com
For bulk book orders and speaking inquiries, email:
info@anthonysanni.com

ACKNOWLEDGEMENTS

If you are here, you are either one of that treasured, gracious, and rare breed of readers who actually reads the authors acknowledgements, or you have contributed in some way to this book and are looking to see if your name is mentioned. In either case, I thank you and I hope you will not be disappointed.

First and above all else, to my lovely wife, **Amaka**: You always believed in me and loved me. But in writing this book, you did a lot of putting up as well. You listened patiently as I soliloquized about my ideas, often at odd times; you picked up the slack whenever I went into a research or writing frenzy; you encouraged me when I, as all writers do at some point, felt despair and doubt. Thank you.

To my editor, **Emily**: Thank you for being a trained and insightful set of eyes—nudging where needed, tweaking where necessary and polishing all around.

To **Darren Sartison** and **Ann Nakaska:** Thank you for giving generously of your time and sharing your insights and your stories. Your contribution added immense value to this work.

To my family: My mother, **Comfort**, and beloved siblings, **Kunle**, **Kemi**, **Bayo** and **Temi**. You helped make me who I am. And since who I am wrote this book, I think you should get credit for doing such a fine job.

To **my father**: Even in death, your life continues to instruct and inspire.

To the **staff of my neighbourhood coffee shop:** We spent many very early hours of the day together. And though you may not have known, every time you asked me how the book was going, you motivated me to get it done, and done well. Thank you.

To **you:** Thanks for reading. I hope you found what you were looking for. Or at least something useful in its stead.

NOTES

Introduction

1. **Trump Tweets:** Article in Quanta Magazine—an independent publication for the enhancement of public knowledge of science—*A Power Law Keeps the Brain's Perceptions Balanced.* In the article, neuroscientist Kenneth Harris of University College London, who has been studying the Power Law, remarked "the distribution of the number of exclamation marks in tweets from Donald Trump follows a power law". In chapter 1 of this book—*The Law of the Vital Few*—the connection is made between The Law of the Vital Few and Power Law.

Chapter 1

2. **Moses Juran quote**: https://www.britannica.com/topic/management-science
3. **Richard Koch reference:** *The 80/20 Principle* book by Richard Koch, (2008) Doubleday. Chapter 2: How to think 80/20. On page 24, Koch states "Of course, the exact relationship may not be 80/20. 80/20 is both a convenient metaphor, and a useful hypothesis, but it is not the only pattern."
4. **Quote form Richard Koch:** *The 80/20 Principle* book by Richard Koch. (2008) Doubleday. Chapter 2: How to think 80/20.
5. **Pareto Principle**: *Cours d'Économie Politique* Professé a l'Université de Lausanne. Vol. I, 1896; Vol. II, 1897. Pareto never used the term "80/20" in this work
6. **The "one percent"**: There are countless articles in different journals in different disciplines from economics to sociology that address the "one percent". A good primer on the topic

I can recommend for reading is a concise review from the Department of Sociology in Duke University: *The One Percent* by Lisa A. Keister. Annu. Rev. Sociol. 2014. 40:347–67.

On the everyday side, a popular film *The One Percent* released in 2006 explores the concept. And for some international context, the news network CNBC published a neat little article as recently as 2019—*Here's How Much Money You Need to Make to be in the Top 1 Percent in 8 Different Countries*: https://www.cnbc.com/2019/03/08/how-much-money-you-need-to-make-to-be-in-the-top-1-percent.html

Interestingly, as further proof of the infallibility of the principle of imbalance, even the top one percent have a top one percent. See: https://review.chicagobooth.edu/economics/2017/article/never-mind-1-percent-lets-talk-about-001-percent

7. **Americans and food emissions**: Popular Science Magazine article by Sarah Chodosh, *One-Fifth of Americans are Responsible for Half the Country's Food-Based Emissions* https://getpocket.com/explore/item/one-fifth-of-americans-are-responsible-for-half-the-country-s-food-based-emissions?utm_source=pocket-newtab

8. **Imbalance of usage of words on languages**: *The Science of Accelerated Learning: Advanced Strategies for Quicker Comprehension, Greater Retention, and Systematic Expertise.* Author: Peter Hollins © Peter Hollins 2018
   In Chapter 7: Hollins draws on the insights of Gabriel Wyner (CEO and Founder of Fluent Forever), Dr. Alexander Alguelles (a notable linguist and polyglot) and Dr. Paul Nation (a language and linguistics researcher) to describe how the Pareto Principle influences language learning.

9. **Procter and Gamble apply Pareto principle**: *Lafley's P&G Brand Cull and the 80/20 Rule.* Article by Michael Schrage on HBR. Published August 4, 2014. https://hbr.org/2014/08/lafleys-pg-brand-cull-and-the-8020-rule Accessed 2020-02-14 @8.28hrs MST; *P&G to sell up to 100 brands to revive sales, cut costs* Reuters Article by Devika Krishner August 4,

2014. https://www.reuters.com/article/us-procter-gamble-results/pg-to-sell-up-to-100-brands-to-revive-sales-cut-costs-idUSKBN0G13WX20140804 Accessed 2020-02-14 at 8:32MST

10. **P&G Annual Reports:** P&G Annual Reports: https://www.pginvestor.com/CustomPage/Index?keyGenPage=1073748359 These are also summarized nicely in an Investopedia article: *Procter & Gamble Trims Down to Ramp Up.* Investopedia by Jason Fernando September 16, 2019.

11. **Etymology of "Activity":** etymonline.com

Chapter 2

12. **World population vs internet users**: Calculated and compared from the following sources: https://www.statista.com/statistics/617136/digital-population-worldwide/ https://www.worldometers.info/world-population/ world-population-by-year/

13. **Nielsen Norman on Wikipedia and 90-9-1**: Article by Nielsen Norman, *The 90-9-1 Rule for Participation Inequality in Social Media and Online Communities* https://www.nngroup.com/articles/participation-inequality/

14. **Quincy Apparel Case**: From Harvard Business Review: HBR —Quincy Apparel (A) - https://store.hbr.org/product/quincy-apparel-a/815067

15. **Business Insider reference on investor behaviour:** Alyson Shontel, Business Insider: https://www.businessinsider.com/after-10-months-a-boatload-of-press-and-a-ceos-departure-apparel-startup-quincy-shuts-down-2013-1 url accessed 2019-12-28 at 11:26MST

Chapter 3

16. **Chapter opening quote from Tony Robbins:** From Tony Robbins' Book, *Awaken the Giant Within: How to Take*

Immediate Control of Your Mental, Emotional, Physical and Financial Destiny!

17. **Michael Phelps quote**: Pg. 5 Prologue of the book *No Limits: The will to succeed* by M. Phelps

18. **Phelps Olympic records**: *The Most Decorated Olympian of all time.* https://www.olympic.org/michael-phelps

19. **Big tech acquisitions**: *The Four: The hidden DNA of Amazon, Apple, Facebook and Google,* Book by Scott Galloway.

20. **History of Shell**: https://www.ektinteractive.com/history-of-oil/https://www.shell.com/about-us/our-heritage/our-company-history.html

Chapter 5

21. **Tree Planting Proverb**: As is common with proverbs, the author of this proverb is unknown. It is popularly referenced as "An Old Chinese Proverb"

Chapter 6

22. **"Future Homer" reference**: Long, T. L. (Writer), & Kruse, N. (Director). (2010). *MoneyBart* [Television series episode]. In A. Jean, J. Frink, J. L. Brooks, M. Groening, M. Selman, & S. Simon (Producers), The Simpsons. Los Angeles, CA: 20th Century Fox Television.

23. **Chip and Dan Heath reference**: The Heath Brothers use the analogy of the rider and elephant for a large portion of their book *Switch.* However, they credit Jonathan Haidt, a social psychologist and Professor of Ethical Leadership at New York University's Stern School of Business, with the analogy in their "Recommendations for Additional Reading" section.

24. **Tim Urban reference**: Tim Urban is the co-founder of the website *Wait but why.* The reference here is to his popular TED Talk *Inside the Mind of a Master Procrastinator* (March 2016) https://www.ted.com/speakers/tim_urban

25. **Plato Reference**: From the dialogue *Phaedrus*

Chapter 7

26. **Link between depression and unemployment:** This is an established connection in clinical psychology. Two useful resources that explicate this are Warr PB. *Twelve questions about unemployment and health.* In: Roberts B, Finnegan R, Gallie D (eds*). New Approaches to Economic Life.* Manchester: Manchester University Press, 1985. And Bartley MJ. *Unemployment and ill health: understanding the relationship.* J Epidemiol Community Health 1994; 48:333 —37.
    Also, if you are wondering if this a chicken and egg situation where people already predisposed to depression are more likely to wind up unemployed, this paper shows that not to be case, at least with young males: Montgomery, S. M., Cook, D. G., Bartley, M. J., & Wadsworth, M. E. (1999). *Unemployment pre-dates symptoms of depression and anxiety resulting in medical consultation in young men.* International Journal of Epidemiology, 28(1), 95-100.

27. **CLEAR Model references**: https://cdn.southampton. ac.uk/assets/imported/transforms/content-block/ UsefulDownloads_Download/59CB199C2A5841 109BF2EA4EA98017B6/GROW-Model.pdf

28. **Bill Withers quote:** From the book *Wisdom* by Andrew Zuckerman

Chapter 8

29. **Dunedin Study publications**: https://dunedinstudy.otago. ac.nz/

30. **Dunedin checkpoint study quote reference**: *A gradient of childhood self-control predicts health, wealth, and public safety.* https://www.pnas.org/content/pnas/108/7/2693.full.pdf

31. **Meg Oaten and Ken Cheng Research on self control**: M. Oaten and K. Cheng, *Improvements in Self-Control from Financial Monitoring,* Journal of Economic Psychology 28 (2006): 487-501.

32. **Research connecting exercise and development of self control:** M. Oaten and K. Cheng, *Longitudinal Gains in Self-Regulation from Regular physical Exercise*, British Journal of Health Psychology 11 (2006):717-33.

33. **Building discipline through discipline exercises**: Other work by the scientists mentioned in this chapter as well as authorities like Dr Baumeister indicate this to be true. See more in Baumeister's book *Willpower*. Also see: Mauraven, M., Baumeister, R., & Tice, D. (1999). *Longitudinal improvement in self-regulation through practice: Building self-control strength through repeated exercise.* Journal of Social Psychology, 139, 446-457

34. **Reddit reference**: What is Reddit? A Beginner's guide to the front page of the internet

Chapter 9

35. **Multiverse, Parallel Universes and decisions**: Sean Carroll's book *Something Deeply Hidden* talks about this idea. A concise reference can be found in an interview with the author by NBC news. Quote from the interview:
"'It's absolutely possible that there are multiple worlds where you made different decisions. We're just obeying the laws of physics," says Sean Carroll, a theoretical physicist at the California Institute of Technology and the author of a new book on many worlds titled "Something Deeply Hidden."'
https://www.nbcnews.com/mach/science/weirdest-idea-quantum-physics-catching-there-may-be-endless-worlds-ncna1068706
You may also see: *Parallel Worlds: A Journey Through Creation, Higher Dimensions, and the Future of the Cosmos* by Michio Kaku (2005). First Anchor Books Ed. The entire book is a fascinating read but the chapter of interest is Chapter 6: Parallel Quantum Universes.

36. **Books on habits and Cue-Routine-Reward feedback Loop**: See the books: *The Power of Habit: Why We do What We Do in Life and Business* by Charles Duhigg; and *Atomic Habits: An*

easy and proven way to build good habits and break bad ones by James Clear.

37. **Implementation Intention study**: Sarah Milne, Sheina Orbell and Paschal Sheeran, *Combining Motivational and Volitional Interventions to Promote Exercise Participation: Protection Motivation Theory and Implementation Intentions* British Journal of Health Psychology 7 (May 2002): 163-184. In the study, about 38 per cent of the members who did not have an implementation intention stuck to their goal of exercising weekly versus 91 percent of those with an articulated implementation intention.

38. **Peak-end Rule reference**: See Chapter 35 of the book *Thinking Fast an*d *Slow* by Daniel Kahneman (2011). Anchor Canada edition published 2013.

Chapter 10

39. **Mindfulness training institute:** TLEX˚ Institute | Transformational Leadership for Excellence Institute: https:// tlexinstitute.com/ Accessed 2019-09-139@14:40MST

40. **Tim Feriss reference**: Tim Feriss Show podcast, Interview with Tom Bilyeu and *Tools of Titans* book by Tim Feriss.

41. **Anti-ageing effects on meditation**: Research from the Spirit Rock Meditation Center in Northern California on lengthening of telomeres. Reported in Time Magazine's Special Issue: *The New Mindfulness*. September/October 2019.

42. **Serotonin, Dopamine and Adrenalin effects**: *The Brain Rules: 12 Principles for surviving and thriving at work, home and school.* By John Medina. Pear Press. 2008. Pg. 202

43. **Serotonin and self-efficacy**: *The Neuroscience of Self-Efficacy: Vertically Integrated Leisure Theory and Its Implications for Theory-Based Programming* by Garrett Anderson Stone https:// js.sagamorepub.com/jorel/article/view/7606

44. **Serotonin and antidepressant medication pharmacology**: Catherine J. Harmer, *Serotonin and Emotional Processing: Does it Help Explain Antidepressant Drug Action?*

Neuropharmacology 55, no. 6 (2008): 1023-28;
Habits of a Happy Brain: Retrain Your Brain to Boost Your Serotonin, Dopamine, Oxytocin, & Endorphin Levels by Loretta Graziano PhD. Adams Media 2005.

45. **Zen meditation study**: Xinjun Yu, Masaki Fumoto, Yasushi Nakatani, Tamami Sekiyama, Hiromi Kikuchi, Yoshinari Seki, Ikuko Sato-Suzuki, Hideho Arita, *Activation of the anterior prefrontal cortex and serotonergic system is associated with improvements in mood and EEG changes induced by Zen meditation practice in novices.* International Journal of Psychophysiology (2011) 103-111

46. **Alpha waves and creativity**: Though many studies have pointed to this connection, this journal publication provides both a convincing argument and a store of related references: Luft, Caroline & Zioga, Ioanna & Thompson, Nicholas & Banissy, Michael & Bhattacharya, Joydeep. (2018). *Right temporal alpha oscillations as a neural mechanism for inhibiting obvious associations.* Proceedings of the National Academy of Sciences. 115.
Quote from the paper's abstract: "These studies altogether indicate that right temporal alpha oscillations may support creativity by acting as a neural mechanism for an active inhibition of obvious semantic associations."

47. **Elephant Documentary**: British Broadcasting Corporation (BBC) TV Series: *Africa* (Episode 2: Savannah) 2013. BBC

48. **Alex Bandura quote**: This quote is from the abstract of Bandura's landmark paper—Bandura, A. (2010). *Self-Efficacy.* In The Corsini Encyclopedia of Psychology (eds I.B. Weiner and W.E. Craighead).

49. **Fixed and Growth Mindsets**: Carol Dweck's book *Mindset: The New Psychology of Success*

50. **Self-efficacy in other species**: Dominic D.P Johnson, J. H. (2011). *The evolution of overconfidence.* Nature, *317-320.*

51. **Quote on changing the world:** The famous quote is by Steve Jobs during an address to Apple as part of the company's 1997 *Think Different* campaign.

Chapter 11

52. **Similarity in DNA of humans and other species:** Human Genome Research Institute: https://www.genome.gov/about-genomics/fact-sheets/Comparative-Genomics-Fact-Sheet

53. **Comparing brain sizes:** Shoshani, J., Kupsky, W.J. and Marchant, G.H., *Elephant brain. Part I: Gross morphology functions, comparative anatomy, and evolution*, Brain Res. Bulletin, 70:124-157, 2006
    Clever ape: https://science.howstuffworks.com/life/inside-the-mind/human-brain/10-brain-myths5.htm

54. **Human brain complexity and higher functions:** Tali Sharot, *The Optimism Bias*. Alfred A Knopff Canada, 2011, Pg. 38.

55. **Communication in Dolphins:** Janik, V.M. & Sayigh, L.S. *Communication in bottlenose dolphins: 50 years of signature whistle research* J Comp Physiol A (2013) 199: 479. https://doi.org/10.1007/s00359-013-0817-7

56. **Steven Pinker Quote:** From the book *The Language Instinct: How the Mind Creates Language.* By Steven Pinker (1994) First Harper Perennial Modern Classics Edition published 2007. See Chapter 1: An Instinct to Acquire an Art.

57. **Nuanced communication in monkeys:** Yuval Noah Harari, *Sapiens.* See Harari's discussion in Chapter 2: The Tree of Knowledge.

58. **"Planning" by other animals:** Tali Sharot, *The Optimism Bias.* Alfred A Knopff Canada, 2011, Pg. 26

59. **Wasp-inspired algorithms:** *Wasp-Inspired Construction Algorithms* by Marcin L. Pilat. Department of Computer Science, University of Calgary.

60. **Wasp nest-construction tampering experiment:** Smith, A.P. (1978). *An investigation of the mechanisms underlying nest construction in the mud wasp.* AnimalBehaviour,26, 232 —240.

61. **Great Apes plan only as well as human toddlers**: Osvath, Mathias & Osvath, Helena. (2008). *Chimpanzee (Pan troglodytes) and orangutan (Pongo abelii) forethought: Self-control and pre-experience in the face of future tool use.* Animal cognition. 11. 661-74. 10.1007/s10071-008-0157-0

62. **Fail to plan quote**: This quote is popularly attributed to United States Founding Father and polymath Benjamin Franklin.

63. **Theories on how the universe might end**: *Parallel Worlds: A Journey Through Creation, Higher Dimensions, and the Future of the Cosmos*—Book by Michio Kaku. Also see the shorter video which summarized the ideas: https://www.youtube.com/watch?v=R5orcCuprG4

64. **Human hand, thumbs and TVF footnote**: Napier JR (1965) *Evolution of the human hand.* Proc. RoyalInst. Great Britain40, 544 —557.

65. **Task time prediction study on graduate students**: Buehler, Roger & Griffin, Dale & Ross, Michael. (1994*). Exploring the "Planning Fallacy": Why People Underestimate Their Task Completion Times.* Journal of Personality and Social Psychology. 67. 366-381. 10.1037/0022-3514.67.3.366.

66. **Original research on Decision making and The Planning Fallacy**: Kahneman, D., & Tversky, A. (1979). *Intuitive prediction: Biases and corrective procedures.* TIMS Studies in Management Science, 12, 313-327.

Chapter 12

67. **Michel de Montaigne quote**: From the essay *On the education of children.* In: "Montaigne's Essay: Top Essays" by Michel de Montaigne. Translated by Charles Cotton.

68. **Simon Sinek Reference**: *Start with Why: How Great Leaders Inspire Everyone to Take Action.* By Simon Sinek. Penguin Books USA.

69. **Seek and you shall find quote**: The words of Jesus as recorded in Matthew Chapter 7 v.7 in the Holy Bible. King

James Version. Full quote is "Ask, and it shall be given you; seek, and ye shall find; knock, and it shall be opened unto you"

Chapter 13

70. **Repetition leads to ease:** See the Stanford Medicine article *Neural activity promotes brain plasticity through myelin growth*: https://med.stanford.edu/news/all-news/2014/04/neural-activity-promotes-brain-plasticity-through-myelin-growth-study-finds.html

71. **100 years for 1 second in the 100m race**: The IAAF records from 1912 to 2016 accessible from the IAAF website. Also, see the BBC Sport article *How Donald Lippincott blazed trail as first 100m record holder* https://www.bbc.com/sport/olympics/18409733

72. **Purposeful Practice Outline**: See the book *Peak: How to Master Almost Anything*. Anders Ericsson and Robert Pool. Penguin Canada 2016. Pg. 22

Chapter 14

73. **Comedy of insights Seinfeld episode**: Seinfeld Episode *The Pool Guy* aired first November 16, 1995. Directed by Andy Ackerman and written by David Mandel. NBC.

74. **Bandwidth—capacity, not speed**: Special thanks to my wife—a certified network specialist turned business consultant for expounding this to me: *No honey, bandwidth is NOT a measure of speed. It is a measure of capacity.* And thanks to Harvey Taphorn who corrected the original numbers breakdown for MB, GB and TB.

75. **Self Determination Theory**: Richard M. Ryan and Edward L. Deci. *Self-Determination Theory: Basic Psychological Needs in Motivation, Development, and Wellness.* Guilford Press (2017)

76. **Gallup Corporation profile**: https://www.britannica.com/topic/Gallup-Organization Accessed 2020-02-11 06:05MST https://www.gallup.com/corporate/212381/who-we-are.aspx Accessed 2020-02-11 06:36am MST

77. **Calculation of time spent at work**: Most North Americans actually sleep less than the prescribed 8 hours but I chose the recommended number here as an optimistic estimate. Usually the sleep deprivation, when present, is linked to spending *more* not less time at work further making my point in the chapter that work relationships matter.

Chapter 15

78. **Comedians opening lines**: Amy Schumer Netflix Special *Growing* opens with "Thank you so much Chicago. Thank you." Aziz Ansari *Buried Alive*: "Thank you so much Philadelphia. Thank you thank you. Wow!" Sebastian Maniscalco, *Stay Hungry*: "Beautiful New York City"

79. **Laughter and social effects:** Work by researchers in the field of laughter like the late neurobiologist and psychologist Dr. Robert Provine have shown that laughter is an inherently social activity we share with people we feel close to or at least connected to in some way. One of the points Dr. Provine makes in his book *Laughter: A Scientific Investigation*, is that laughter is a social glue that draws group members into the fold.

80. **Loose connections and social change:** *The Power of Habit: Why We do What We Do in Life and Business* by Charles Duhigg;
    G. Davis, D. McAdam, and W. Scott, *Social Movements and Organizations*. New York: Cambridge University, 2005.

81. **Giver, receiver and observer benefit from kindness**: See Haidt, J. (2003). *Elevation and the positive psychology of morality.* In C. L. M. Keyes & J. Haidt (Eds.) Flourishing: Positive psychology and the life well-lived. Washington DC: American Psychological Association. (pp. 275-289).
    Dr Steve Taylor, professor of psychology in Leeds, also has a good article specifically discussing the benefits to witnessing kind acts. *Elation: The Amazing Effect of Witnessing Acts of Kindness*: https://www.psychologytoday.com/ca/

blog/out-the-darkness/201311/elation-the-amazing-effec
t-witnessing-acts-kindness-0?quicktabs_5=0

82. **Emmet Fox quote**: *The Sermon on the Mount: The Key to Success in Life* by Emmet Fox. HarperCollins NY. Pg 138. Fox's words: "You do not owe an atom of loyalty to anyone or anything in the universe except your own Indwelling Christ." The term "Indwelling Christ" is one Fox used often to represent the spiritual sovereignty he believed, as I do, resides in every human being.

INDEX

Made in the USA
Middletown, DE
05 May 2022

65321390R10142